NOTHING *to* LOSE *but* MY LIFE

A MEMOIR

DAVID WIENER

Nothing to Lose But My Life: A Memoir

ISBN 979-8-9937369-1-4 (paperback)
ISBN 979-8-9937369-0-7 (eBook)

Second edition

Library of Congress Control Number on file.

Publication managed by AuthorImprints.com

Dedicated to
The memory of my brothers and sisters and my
beloved parents, Moshe Chaim and Chana Sura

And to
My wonderful family and the memory of my wife of 50 years, Renée

Never say you are walking your final road Though leaden skies conceal the days of blue. Our steps will beat out like drums

We are here!

We are coming with all our pain and all our woe. That our might and our courage will sprout again. Our enemy will vanish and fade away.

From generation to generation let them be singing this song.

This song is written in blood not in pencil-lead. It is not sung by the free–flying birds overhead but a people stood among collapsing walls

*And sang this song with pistols in their hand. **

"The Partisan Song (Zog Nit Keyn Mol!)"
by Hirsch Glick (1922–1944)

*I learned this song in May 1944 while in the Deblin work camp.

CONTENTS

18 Years Later

Eighteen years have passed since I first shared my story with the world. At the time, I believed I was writing the final chapters of a long and extraordinary life—a life shaped by survival, shadowed by unimaginable loss, and uplifted by love, perseverance, and purpose.

But here I am at 99 years young, realizing there was still more to write.

Since the last edition of this book, I have walked through both joy and sorrow many times. My beloved second wife—whose love and devotion sustained me through some of my darkest and brightest days—passed away from cancer. Her loss left a silence in my life that words cannot fill. And yet, life—persistent and resilient—moved forward, and so did I. In time, I remarried. Not to replace what was lost, but to find companionship once more. To not be alone.

There have also been moments of triumph—the kind that would have seemed impossible to the boy I once was: the boy who ran from Nazi soldiers, who watched his dreams reduced to ash, who was told he had no future. Today, I can proudly say that two of my four grandchildren, Mathieu and Shane, have earned law degrees. Their achievements are not only reflections of their brilliance and dedication—they are living proof of the unbroken line of hope that stretches across generations.

And perhaps most humbling of all: I received an honorary law degree from Pepperdine University's School of Law. Pepperdine recognized my lifetime of advocacy, philanthropy, and unwavering belief in staying hopeful—even in the face of overwhelming darkness. For me, the honor reached far deeper than ceremony. It was the fulfillment of a dream born in a time when dreaming was forbidden for people like me. The Nazis tried to erase us—our families, our culture, our future—and they nearly succeeded.

Standing on that stage in academic robes, receiving the degree they swore would never be mine, felt like vindication. They took everything— but not my will. Not my dreams. Not my belief in the power of education, in the strength of family, in helping others, and in life itself.

This updated edition is not merely a continuation of my story—it is a testament to survival, to new beginnings, and to the enduring power of dreams that refuse to die. My father always told me: *"Never give up, and never give in."* His words carried me through the most horrific times. Over the years, I developed a credo of my own, one I've passed down to my children and grandchildren:

"If there's a will, there's a way."

And:

"If you can do it, I can do it. It may take me a little longer, and I may have to work a little harder—but I will get there."

I offer these pages now with deeper gratitude, sharper clarity, and a heart still full of wonder. Life, it turns out, had much more to teach me— and perhaps, still has more to teach us all.

—David Wiener

chapter one

A LOVING AND
CARING FAMILY

On May 14, 1926, Marshal Josef Pilsudski staged a military coup and overthrew the elected government of Poland. He was revered as a hero and his fellow countrymen credited him with reunifying the country and bringing about its true independence from domination by its German and Russian neighbors who fought over Poland like two mastiffs tearing at a slab of bloody meat. Pilsudski trained his troops to believe that "To be defeated and not to submit, that is victory; to be victorious and rest on one's laurels, that is defeat." He infused Poland with a sense of pride and helped to rehabilitate its people from the devastating blows that it suffered during and after World War I. He took the title of Minister of Defense in charge of the country's army which numbered 450,000 soldiers, leaving the running of the country to a new president and prime minister. Despite his infectious optimism and his political cunning, Marshal Piilsudski would later prove no match against Germany and Russia who had colluded to slice up Poland, once again ending a period of illusory confidence.

I was born just a few days after Pilsudski's coup d'etat, on May 30, 1926 in Lodz, Poland, southwest of the capital, Warsaw. Lodz had the largest textile industry in Europe and more than 50 percent of the Jewish population was employed in one way or another in that industry. At the time, Jews accounted for more than 30 percent of Lodz' population. Many of these Jews came to Lodz from other parts of Eastern Europe and Russia to escape vicious persecution.

My father, Moszek (Moshe) Chaim Wiener, was born in Lublin, a city in the southeastern part of Poland, where he lived until after World War I when he moved to Lodz. Lublin was an important center of Jewish religion, education, and social life, with many synagogues, a Jewish hospital and orphanage, a shelter for the elderly, and Jewish schools and newspapers. To the east of Lublin were thick forests that reached to the border of the Ukraine. Both my father and grandfather were graduates of the Yeshiva in Lublin and were devoted Jewish scholars, studying Torah and Talmud and praying daily. My grandfather made his living as a lumber broker and it is said that he was both a prosperous businessman and a devout Jew. My father's younger brother, Aaron, and our family used to visit one another on Saturday evenings after Shabbat and on the Jewish holidays. Uncle Aaron's son was a real genius, and was fluent in many languages. To our family's great sadness, my cousin died when he was only 17 years old, before the start of World War II.

Shortly before my father moved to Lodz, he married my mother, Hanche (Hannah) Sura Makler who lived outside Lublin. She was reputed to be the most beautiful girl in her village and my father, who was an exceedingly proud man, must have felt very fortunate to marry her. Theirs was an arranged marriage, which was customary at the time. My father was 19 years old and my mother was 16. By today's standards, that seems very young, but considering the expectation that children would become independent of their parents and self-supporting, often before they were 20 years old, it was not unusual. After my parents married, Hannah's mother moved to Deblin, Poland. My mother had two sisters–Pearl, who married Aaron Gilbert, and a younger sister, living in Warsaw. All three sisters had smiles like a million dollars.

My father was a Talmud teacher in Lodz and a disciple of the famous and charismatic Hasidic Gerer Rebbe, Abraham Mordecai Alter. My mother had a small yard goods store where she worked until my mother and father were blessed with a family of nine children. Every two years a child was born to Moshe and Hannah—Yankel (Jacob), Szyje, Yitzchak,

Malka (my only sister), Yosel, Yidel, Wolf, Myself, and the baby, Mendel. I was the second to the youngest child. There was an 18-year difference from the oldest to the youngest child—double chai—which should have guaranteed good fortune and a long life for our family, but that was not to be.

Our family lived in a one-room apartment on the top floor of a seven-story building in Lodz on Ul Wolborska 18. The room was "all purpose" and it was for sleeping, eating, studying, and entertaining friends and family. The only reason that it was not unbearably overcrowded is that as soon as a son was old enough to fend for himself, like a little bird, he would leave the nest and find another place to live. And once he left, each son always donated money to the family to help support the younger children. By the time I was born, there were only four children in our apartment. My father was 41 and my mother was 36.

Right next door, at Ul Wolborska 20, was Lodz' oldest Orthodox synagogue. Known as the "Altshtot" synagogue, it was an imposing stone building which contained not one, but two women's galleries above the main sanctuary where the men sat. There were 1,500 seats, more than 30 Torah scrolls in the Ark, and many silver ornaments and ancient works of Judaica. Down the street was the outdoor market where peddlers sold their wares and farmers brought their produce to sell to Lodz' growing population. There were almost 100,000 Jews who made up a bustling and thriving community.

Every morning, my father left for synagogue, wrapped his left arm in teffilin and recited the Sh'ma before assuming his teaching duties at the synagogue. In the evening he would pray twice—once at sunset and again when the stars came out. I remember sitting on his lap on the steps in front of the synagogue waiting for the sun to set, drinking soda water and playing with his long, black beard. These were happy times.

Every Friday night, my sister, Malka, would bathe me and then we would all welcome the Sabbath. Usually, there were at least nine members of the family around the table since my older brothers who had left would come home to celebrate Shabbat with my parents. My mother was truly the Sabbath queen; with tears in her eyes, she would take in the magnificent sight of her family, and the contented and pious countenance of my father,

Moshe. We had very little in the way of possessions; whatever food was put on the table was sufficient, and we were always taught to "be happy in our lives and content with what we were given and look toward the future." Our family was filled with love and warmth.

On Saturday mornings, at six o'clock, my father would leave our apartment, and read the Torah as part of Shabbat services before a congregation of more than 200 Hasidic Jews in the main sanctuary of the synagogue next door. Over the course of the morning the synagogue filled with worshippers from our neighborhood.

My parents isolated us from rumors that something terrible was going to happen to the Jews. They used to tell us that God would take care of everything. When Vladimir (Ze'ev) Jabotinksy came to Poland espousing Zionism and carrying the message that a "fire is burning" in Europe, my parents simply pulled in their haunches and reverted to unquestioning faith in the Almighty. They did not listen to Jabotinsky's urgings that Jews immigrate to Palestine where they might establish a safe and secure Jewish homeland. For my parents, Lodz was home. After all, my father could see his beautiful synagogue from our apartment and that was where his world began and ended.

Up until the time that I was eight or nine I attended the local heider. I didn't study very hard because all the subjects came easily to me. I was a restless child and looked forward to playing soccer in the streets with friends after school. Although I was small for my age, I was a pretty good player until I started having trouble breathing. The doctor discovered that I had tuberculosis which was not unusual since the air in Lodz was filthy dirty from the factory fumes.

My parents sent me to live with my oldest brother, Jacob, and his wife, Irene. They lived in Krotoszyn, a small town in the province of Posznan to the west of Lodz near the German border. The air was much cleaner there, and my brother and his wife took very good care of me. My brother, who was a textile salesman, was doing very well—he had a house and a car. His wife was a German Jew and her father was a cantor who sang in the synagogue next to the house where we lived. The congregation was made up exclusively of Jewish soldiers in the Polish army who were stationed in the region.

Jacob and Irene had no children and they treated me as if I were their own son. When I came to live with them they gave me a bicycle which was a real luxury. Every Passover, they bought me a new, custom-made suit for the holiday. I used to come home to visit my parents during summer vacations and on Rosh Hashanah and Yom Kippur. Otherwise, I stayed in Krotoszyn.

We were one of only four Jewish families living in Krotoszyn. The history of the town is one of annexation and changes in nationality that led to the disappearance of the Jewish population. For a time, Krotoszyn was a part of Prussia and aligned itself with Germany. After World War I, the town became part of Poland. According to YIVO's Institute for Social Research, by the eve of World War I, there were only 411 Jews left in the town. Most of the Jews who had lived there had emigrated to Germany, the United States, or even to South America. Krotoszyn was a lonely place to be a Jew, especially after I experienced the vibrant Jewish life of Lodz. Most of its residents were Catholic and spoke German and Polish as a result of its history of annexation.

There was no Jewish day school in the town, and so I went to the local public school which was named after Marshal Josef Pilsudski. All the classes were taught in Polish, and when I arrived I only spoke Yiddish which was the language spoken in my parents' home and in our neighborhood, but somehow I excelled in my studies and when I was given a test to determine what grade I should be in, I was pushed ahead two grades. Although I was the youngest child in my class, I adapted to my circumstances because I was a very serious student and wanted to get ahead so that I could qualify for a university education.

Most of my fellow students were Catholic and they attended religious classes every day. Because I was Jewish I was excused from class. One day, my best friend said to me, "I don't want to talk to you anymore."

I was dumbfounded, "Why?"

"Because you killed Jesus." That is what my classmates were being taught in religious school. I ended up getting into a lot of fights. One time, two boys were waiting for me outside class. One kid jumped me. I had a heavy satchel full of books and I hit him hard on the head; I swung the satchel around and knocked the other kid's teeth out. The next day, one of the boys went to the principal to complain and I was yanked into his office. The principal hit me over the head and struck my hands with a ruler as punishment. Strange to tell, one of the boys, Josef Kowalski, became my best friend. He was really dumb and I did him a favor by tutoring him in Polish history and math so he protected me from the other boys. He was a big guy and the other bullies did not want to get into a fight with him.

But I had to put up with other forms of "torture" at school. Our math teacher had to go away on occasion, and I was asked to take over the class for a while since I was the top student. Eventually, we got a new teacher, Mr. Leonovich, and he taught us division. He'd call on one, two, three students to solve a problem, and none of them could come up with the right answer. I would raise my hand to get the teacher's attention.

"O.K. David, what is the correct answer?"

I stood up, went to the blackboard, and one, two, three, I solved the problem. I turned around to go back to my seat. Mr. Leonovich said, "No, David, stand here." He told the class, "Look carefully at this guy. He's a Jew (Zydek). When you grow up, and you want to buy something from him, he's clever enough that he will know how to cheat you." I will never forget that moment for the rest of my life. When I told my brother, Jacob, what had happened, he said, "Just ignore them." Being Jewish in a Catholic town, made us vulnerable to persecution, and my brother did not think that the situation warranted going to the principal. Besides, I think that he knew that the outcome would not be in my favor, and he was right.

Twice a week, after school, I took violin lessons from a music teacher, Mr. Wallace, a Polish German who was secretly spying on the Polish army for the Nazis. He seemed like a very nice guy, and he was a good teacher. He was very demanding and didn't take any nonsense from his pupils. He always dressed very well, and had a full head of brown hair. I used to go to his apartment which was right next to the Polish army headquarters in Krotoszyn. I practiced very hard, and loved to play the music of Mozart and Schumann. My brother, Jacob, also played the violin and we would sometimes play duets together. It was lovely. My brother also had a beautiful singing voice.

A few years later, during the war, I saw Mr. Wallace in the Warsaw ghetto. I ran up to him yelling, "Mr. Wallace! Mr. Wallace!" I was so happy to see him. He warned me, "Stay away from me. I am with the Gestapo." He told me he had been spying on the Polish army headquarters for the Germans all the time that I was taking violin lessons with him. Krotoszyn was full of Germans because the town had been taken over by the Germans after World War I. Many Germans settled there and cooperated with the German government's intelligence department in preparation for an eventual attack on Poland. Mr. Wallace used to pass information to the Germans about the strength of the Polish army and its capacity to stop an invasion. We were soon to learn that the strength of the Polish army was virtually non-existent; it was under-manned and under-equipped to stop the Nazi juggernaut despite Marshal Pilsudski's military acumen. If you have nothing to fight with it's pretty difficult to win a war.

chapter two

THE WAR BEGINS

During the summer of 1939, we were all on pins and needles waiting to see what was going to happen. Rumors were flying that a German invasion of Poland was imminent. The German military was a formidable force, compared to the paltry Polish military which had little equipment and ammunition. I remember a few months before Easter vacation my teacher came into our classroom and announced, "We are going to have a war with Germany." He then said, "If any of you has a bicycle, give it to the Polish army." I was very proud of myself for turning over my precious bicycle to the Polish officials so that they could fight the Germans. My teacher gave me a piece of yellow paper so that when the war was over, I could be "reimbursed" by the government. My brother, Jacob, donated his beautiful white horse. Of course, these gestures proved entirely futile, but at 12 years old, it was impossible for me to imagine what lay ahead for my family, and for the Jewish people of Poland and Europe.

I left Krotoszyn in June 1939 at the end of the school year. The town was only seven miles from the German border, and my parents believed that it was safer for me to be back with them in Lodz. We knew that the war would begin any day. Time seemed to stop and everyone just waited for what seemed like an eternity. On September 1, 1939 Germany declared war on Poland, and within six weeks the German Vermacht completely annihilated any resistance that the Polish army mobilized in defense of the country—then on September 17, the Soviet Union invaded eastern Poland, thus partitioning the country once again.

Every day German tanks rolled through the streets of Lodz. Our apartment building shook from the rumble of the tanks and the motorcycles. The sound of barking dogs pierced the air that was acrid from the smell of gunpowder.

On November 16, I was standing next to our apartment building, and our synagogue was dynamited and completely destroyed by fire right in front of me. Debris from the blast flew everywhere. I really don't know how I survived, but that was just the first of many incidents over the ensuing years when I narrowly escaped death. I watched through the night as the synagogue burned to the ground and with it the precious Torahs, the bimah, and the relics of Judaism that had been the lifeblood of my father's days and years. The destruction of the synagogue was a body blow from which my father did not recover—his whole life was his family and the synagogue.

The Gestapo created a ghetto in Lodz where the Jews were herded like a flock of sheep. The city was renamed Litmannstadt. Jews were forced to wear armbands with a yellow star on our sleeves marking us as Juden. As soon as the Germans occupied the city, all Jewish bank accounts were frozen and Jewish cash holdings were restricted to 2,000 zlotys (the equivalent of $377). Jews could no longer work in the textile industry or other enterprises and all Jewish businesses were turned over to the Germans to pay for the war effort. Jews were seen as a "cash cow" to feed the German war machine. And as an added humiliation and punishment, Jews were forbidden to use public transportation. Jews were not permitted to leave Lodz without the approval of the occupying German army. Synagogue services were shut down and despite religious beliefs, Jews had to keep their shops open on the Sabbath and Jewish holidays. They also had to put a Jewish star in the window of their shops. Jews lived in increasingly squalid and crowded conditions causing disease to spread throughout the ghetto. In the meantime, Germany and its allies moved into the apartments and houses that had been abandoned by the Jews, as part of their campaign to claim Lebensraum (living space) for their country. The Germans did not completely liquidate the Lodz ghetto until July 1944, almost a year before the war finally ended in Europe.

Before the war began, three of my brothers—Yankel (Jacob), Szyje, and Yidel—left Lodz and fled to Bialystok in the Polish Russian zone. They knew things were bad and they figured if they got out, they could come back and get the rest of the family. By this time, my sister, Malka, who was 18 years old, had moved to her own apartment with her husband, Rachmil Schwartz, a tailor. I wanted to go with my brothers, but they said, "We'll come back and get you and the rest of the family. Stay with mother and father." But the border closed in 1940 and they were unable to get back into Poland to try and save us.

In the midst of this turmoil, I turned 13 years old. Normally, I would have had my bar mitzvah, but under the circumstances it was impossible. All I thought about was escaping from the misery and degradation that I saw around me. One day, Heinrich Himmler, himself, passed me on the street. Someone told me who he was, the commander of the SS and one of Nazi Germany's most powerful men. He was a human death machine dressed in a decorated army uniform who would eventually be put in charge of running the Nazi concentration camps to exterminate all Jews and other "undesirables."

I marked my 13th year by escaping the Lodz ghetto three weeks after the synagogue burned down. I think that I had the intention of eventually crossing the border into Russia to be reunited with my brothers. My father was unable to say goodbye to me. It was too much for him to bear seeing his second youngest son leaving home. And with tears running down her beautiful face, my mother's last words to me were, "God bless you my child. Go and be safe." That would be the last time that I ever saw my parents, Moshe Chaim and Hannah Wiener.

My parents had given me enough money to buy a train ticket from Lodz to Warsaw where I planned to stay with my mother's sister. One of my friends and I made the three-hour journey together. He was going to stay with his grandfather who owned a bakery in Warsaw. I found my aunt living at Ul Wronia 19. She was married and had two sons and a daughter who was married to a scholar of psychiatry. My aunt let me sleep on a table, and I worked for her daughter during the day. She had a little swap meet where she sold sugar and dough for bread. I was more or less what you would call a stock boy and I was grateful to have a place to stay in return for the work that I did.

I had been in Warsaw only a few weeks when the Germans established a ghetto in the predominantly Jewish districts of Murandow and Mirow, west of the city center. The ghetto was sealed off by a high brick wall— almost 450,000 Jews from the city and surrounding areas were crammed into the ghetto, and it eventually became the largest ghetto in all of eastern Europe. Living conditions were unbearable. The crowding created disease and filth, and the Jews were prohibited from returning to their homes to get even the most modest of provisions or furniture. Whatever the Germans could get their hands on, they took for their own use—carpets, bedding, tapestries, paintings, even pots and pans.

My aunt's husband and their sons were very religious and every day they would put on teffilin and pray. I was expected to do the same. As I wrapped the teffilin around the fingers of my left hand, I prayed "If God exists, take me right now. I have had enough." I was tired of living.

I looked at the window covered with ice and my image came back to me—a young boy with sunken eyes filled with tears and an expression of sheer resignation. As I recited the Sh'ma, my breath hung in the air from the bitter cold. I can honestly say that my heart was numb, frozen like the ground outside. I had already seen too much suffering and I really saw no point in continuing to live. I prayed that if God really existed he would end my life—that would be my proof that there was a God, but He had other plans for me and my prayers went unanswered.

I left my aunt's house and moved in with my father's first cousin, Waizer, who had two daughters. They lived at Ul Zelazna 33 in another part of the Warsaw ghetto. One of Waizer's daughters was attending gymnasium, and the other daughter was married and living with the family and her two children. I remember walking on Dzielna Street and a young girl standing on the corner offered me her body in exchange for a piece of bread so that her parents could survive. She was probably not more than 15 or 16 years old. Everyone was starving and desperate for food.

One day I saw a man dressed in black with a long beard being lifted into a German ambulance. When people heard the commotion, they came out of their apartments and gathered in the street. I overheard someone shout, "That is the Gerer Rebbe, Abraham Mordecai Alter," who had been my father's spiritual leader. I stood there in a state of shock as the ambulance drove away. I learned that he had "magically" escaped Poland and established a religious center in Jerusalem, and embraced Zionism, after years of preaching that Hasidic Jews should remain in Poland where they would be safe. Whenever I have told other survivors that I saw the Gerer Rebbe with my own eyes in the Warsaw ghetto, they have argued with me, but the YIVO Institute has confirmed that these are the facts.

The streets of the ghetto were strewn with dead bodies covered with brown paper because no one took the time to remove them. Many nights I slept on the ground inside the entrance to an apartment building on Ul Leszno. My entire body was swollen from hunger and my hands and feet were frozen, but I was hardly aware of the cold. I still had on the same blue corduroy suit that I wore on the day that I escaped from the Lodz ghetto. I did not take this suit off my back—which had been given to me by my brother, Jacob and Irene—until 1941 when I "traded" it in for prison garb. My feet were growing and the only way that I could still wear my shoes was to cut off the front tips to make room for my toes. I was not alone in my misery; there were hundreds of other homeless young boys and girls without their parents living on the streets.

Fortuitously, I ran into my friend who escaped from Lodz with me. He said, "David, let me help you out." He took me to his grandfather's bakery where they were making matzos for Pesach. I slept on the stove which was still warm from the day's baking. Slowly I got my strength back after sleeping in the streets for some time—I cannot remember for how long.

I knew that I had to escape the Warsaw ghetto, no matter how great the risk. My life did not mean anything to me anyhow. Someone pushed me over the ghetto wall. I never knew who it was. If the Germans—who were guarding the perimeter—had seen me they would have shot me on the spot, but somehow I slipped by the snarling dogs and the loaded guns.

I found my way to the Warsaw railroad station. Two young ladies were sitting on a bench with a blanket covering their laps. They signaled to me with their fingers to come over to them and asked, "Are you Zydek? Are you Jewish?" I said yes although I was taking a chance because there was no guarantee that they would show me any mercy. Besides, at that point I didn't care if I lived or died. The Gestapo was everywhere with hound dogs patrolling the station to find anyone who might try and escape. The ladies told me to put my head on their breasts and hide under their blanket. Somehow the Gestapo did not discover me. One of the ladies bought me a train ticket to Deblin, near Lublin in Eastern Poland where my mother's sister, Pearl Gilbert lived.

The train was crowded with Germans and Poles moving from place to place. As I boarded the train, a Gestapo officer stopped me. "Where are you going?"

"To see my grandmother." "Where is your passport?"

I told him, "I left it at my grandmother's house." Somehow he bought my story, and because I spoke German to him he let me go.

I knew Pearl's address in Deblin—Ul Okulna 52—which had become part of the Jewish ghetto. She lived there with her husband, Aaron, and her son Abraham Gilbert and her daughter. When I got there, the door opened for me right away. They had a little wooden house and a bed for me in one corner of their "all purpose" room.

Within a few days I was assigned by the Judenrat (the Jewish Council) to work for the Gestapo. Since I was an outsider, the Council picked me to do the heaviest jobs. The Germans were building roads, and I had to unload coal and cement from the trains. At 15, I could work hard and I knew that if I fell down on the job, that would be the end for me. I'd work from six o'clock in the morning until ten o'clock at night, sometimes carrying 100-pound bags of cement on my back in the pouring rain, which made the bags even heavier and the ground slippery from the mud puddles. Many days, I had nothing to eat but I still had to keep on going.

Looking back, I really don't know how I survived. I think, at that point, I discovered the will to live. I wanted to be able to say, "See, somebody survived this horror. Somehow I am here. They couldn't kill me." Furthermore, I hoped that I would be reunited with my family, see my Mother's beautiful smile, and that I would find someone who had survived. I did not yet know the fate of any of my siblings or my parents.

There were also signs that the war might be turning against Germany. Hitler and his generals had made the fatal mistake of invading Russia to the east in June 1941 while simultaneously fighting on the western front. This decision was fortuitous for our survival. The Germans did not bargain for the treacherous cold and the strength of the Russian resistance. They also came up against a citizens' underground that had mobilized behind Russian lines and joined in the fighting against their bitter enemy, the Germans. By the end of 1941, the Russians were able to regain control of Stalingrad from the Germans. In my opinion, this was the turning point of the war and led to the eventual defeat of the Nazis.

And there was another important factor that changed the balance of power of World War II. After hanging back for almost two years, the Americans finally decided to enter the war. Pushed by the attack of the Japanese on Pearl Harbor, the Americans mobilized their sophisticated and formidable air power against Germany who was allied with the Japanese. American troops also joined the Allies on the ground, and ultimately turned the tide of the war against Germany. But the war would go on for another four years.

I was assigned to "cement detail" in Deblin by the Gestapo for about a year and then I was transferred to another group of teenagers who were building a bunker for the Gestapo officers just outside the ghetto. One day, a Polish foreman working for the Germans was mixing cement and he hit one of the Jewish boys. A Gestapo officer, named Edek who was a Polish German, saw the melee. He asked me, "What is going on here?"

Since I was fluent in German and Polish, I was able to answer him, "The foreman doesn't want to work." Edek asked me if I could mix cement. I said yes. I never said no to anything. I also told the boys that were working with me, "Let's not play around. Let's show them we can do the work too." We almost finished the job.

There was also a German Ober Fuhrer Knaphaider. He noticed how hard I was working and that I spoke German so he left me alone. Others he hit with a bat. He didn't need a reason—he just might not like your face or your expression—the smallest provocation and the bat would come out and someone would be covered in his own blood, and have to keep working or face certain death.

During the winter of 1942, I was selected by the Jewish Council to work on building a railroad into Deblin. Everyday, I thought that it was to be the last day of my life. It was bitter cold—the snow and fog were so thick that I could not see 100 feet in front of me. I had no gloves and the flesh on my hands stuck to the ice-cold railroad tracks. The wind was ferocious, blowing snow into my nostrils so that it was hard to breathe. But I had to keep on working or die.

I was bent over fitting the wooden trestles between the train tracks and a locomotive moving slowly along the freshly laid tracks crashed into me, hitting me in the head. I was knocked unconscious. A couple of the men lifted me up onto a stretcher. As I lay there feeling no pain because I probably had gone into shock, one of the men said, "Why should we carry the Jew? Let's just throw him into the locomotive coal bin and let him burn." And then I heard one of the men argue, "No, I know where the kid lives. Let's take him home." They carried me to my Aunt Pearl's house.

I was shaking all over and running a fever of 105 degrees. Aunt Pearl filled a cow bladder with ice and put it on my head to try to bring the swelling down. She was up day and night praying that I would somehow survive. She would never have forgiven herself if her sister's son died in her house. She was truly an angel the way she took care of me.

I remember that a Jewish doctor named Kafka was summoned. He looked at me and said that there was really no use in trying to save me— surely I was going to die because my head injury was so severe. And at that time, human life was worth less than a penny. But the family would not give up on me. Pearl's son, Abraham, found a gentile doctor who agreed to come to the house under the cover of night because he did not want to be seen entering the ghetto. He told my aunt, "If the boy survives the next two days, he will live." The doctor had no medicine, but he gave me hope which is probably why I did not die right then and there.

My aunt stayed up 24-hours a day taking care of me, covering me with blankets and filling the cow bladder with fresh ice from the cellar to bring down the swelling. Eventually my fever broke but I could not turn my head for a month—my neck was stiff as a board. Sixty years later, I still have pain in my neck and a scar on the back of my head from where the locomotive hit me.

When I was strong enough to go out on the street, my friends looked at me as if they were seeing a ghost. "Is that really you?" They could not believe that I was alive; some kids actually ran away from me and others wanted to touch me to make sure that I was human. I felt like I had come back from Hell. I kept repeating my name, "Yes, it is me, Dufce Wiener from Lodz."

The Gestapo announced the liquidation of the Deblin ghetto. The Jews were to be moved to undisclosed locations although there were Jews that heard about the German extermination camps, "the final solution" to the eradication of the Jewish people. It wasn't bad enough that Jews were starving in the ghettos, but now they would face systematic and deliberate murder. Those Jews—the strong, the young—might temporarily escape the concentration camps and be commandeered to a slave labor camp. But once a worker could no longer perform his job, his death was guaranteed.

The Jewish Council was instructed by the Germans to order the Jews in the ghetto to gather in the central marketplace at six o'clock in the morning to begin the liquidation process. A huge crowd appeared with small suit-cases carrying what little they could gather in the few hours that they had been given. We were all naïve and thought that we were going to another work camp. How wrong we were.

People were commanded to go to the left or to the right. I was put in the left line. The Gestapo were hitting those people in the left line, and their dogs were attacking anyone who tried to step out.

All of a sudden *Ober Fuhrer* Knaphaider saw me and said, "What are you doing in the left line?"

I answered, "The *Judenrat* put me in this line."

He yelled, "Raus, Raus," go to the right. "Get out of this line." I later learned that anyone in the left line was transported to Treblinka near Lub-lin. Hidden in the midst of a verdant pine forest, this was the Nazis' second largest concentration camp. Between July 1942 and August 1943 thousands of people, mostly Jews, were murdered in the camp's gas chambers every day while the camp was fully operational.

Standing in the right line, I pointed to my cousin Abraham Gilbert, who was still in the left line. "Herr Knaphaider, that is my cousin. I'd like to have him stand next to me." I managed to save my cousin's life and the two of us were assigned to a work camp in Deblin. My Aunt Pearl and her husband remained in the left line and perished in Treblinka.

The Germans needed labor to build an airport, roads, and a complete infrastructure to carry out the war effort. My hands were covered in calluses and cuts to carry out their dirty work. At one point I was lucky enough to be assigned to kitchen duty. At least it was warm inside and I could sneak some extra food when no one was watching, but this "respite" was to be short-lived.

chapter three

My Name Is Josef Kowalski

By 1944, the Russians were advancing across Poland's eastern front, coming close to Lublin to the north. We suspected that the war might be nearing an end. Those German soldiers who were sent to the Russian front knew that their chances of staying alive were practically zero. I saw German soldiers actually crying like babies when they got their orders to go east into Russia. For an instant the Vermacht soldiers resembled human beings, not simply cogs in a horrific killing machine.

While I was in the Deblin work camp, I had to clean the Gestapo officers' quarters. I saw a pistol hanging in a holster on the top bunk of a double-decker bed. I stole the gun and hid it under a pile of coal. An officer discovered that the gun was missing, and since I had been cleaning the sleeping quarters, I was immediately suspected of having stolen the gun. The officer—whose name was Braun—ordered me to take my shirt off and he beat me with his whip over and over again. Between strikes, I yelled, "I don't know anything about the gun." The beatings finally stopped.

Then the officer turned on Moshe Salzman, who had been working with me, and beat the hell out of him. He begged them to stop and swore that he was innocent. He still carries the scars of that interrogation, but he survived. Luckily Moshe did not know that I had taken the gun because he might have told the Gestapo and they would have probably hanged both of us.

The next day I went back to work and when no one was looking I uncovered the gun in the coal bin, took it back to camp, and hid it. I figured that it could be of some use if I tried to escape. I had nothing to lose since it was a near certainty that the Gestapo planned to kill us within days because the war was turning in favor of the Allies, and the Germans smelled defeat.

Some of my friends in the work camp did try to escape. The Gestapo caught them and hung them from a tree in the middle of camp. Within three days, their skin had turned black as coal. I had to walk right in front of them on my way to work and back. There was no way to avoid the sight of their corpses swinging in the wind. The Gestapo knew that these dead bodies would serve as a warning for anyone planning to escape from the camp.

We heard rumors that the Gestapo was going to liquidate the camp in a couple of days since the Russians were advancing further into Poland and the Allies had launched numerous successful air strikes over German cities.

The Gestapo moved us into a cattle car to be transported out of Deblin. We did not know where we were headed but I knew I had to escape. The train stopped for a few minutes in Czestochowa. My friend, Avram Cohen, and I jumped from the train and in a split second the Gestapo saw us and yelled "Halt, Halt." The first thing I did was throw the gun away. Had they found me with a gun they would have suspected that I was part of the Partisan resistance, and both Avram and I would have been killed. How else would I have had a gun?

Avram and I fell to the ground. One of the Gestapo officers stuck a rifle butt into the side of my head. I could hear the trigger being cocked. My only wish was that he should just shoot me in the head and end this living Hell. I had no time to be afraid. And then one of the Gestapo said, "No, don't shoot him. The bullet is too expensive. Don't waste it on him." They told us to get up and we were taken to the jail in Czestochowa. Somewhere a gramophone was playing a familiar German song, "Meine Heine Sterner," "My Dear Little Star." The two Gestapo started beating me again and said, "Where are you going?"

"We are going to visit our grandparents who live on a little farm not far from here."

"What is your name?"

In a split second, I answered, "My name is Josef Kowalski." That was pure Polish Catholic and the name of my best friend in school. The two men beat Avram and me and threw us into a cellar beneath the jail. There was almost no air to breathe. I could see rain falling throughout the night from a little grate near the ceiling and the dampness was leaching through the walls into puddles on the dirt floor.

After a few days, we were moved into a jail cell. There was another guy in the cell with us. At first we were afraid to say anything to him because we didn't know if we could trust him. After a while I asked him, "Am hu?" (Are you Jewish?). He said yes and told us that his name was Orbach. He was a tall guy and he was from Czestochowa so he knew what was going on. He told us that every three days the Germans picked up the prisoners from the jail.

"Those who go to the left end up at the cemetery and they immediately shoot you and throw you into an open grave. Those who go to the right are taken to the railroad station and on to Auschwitz."

The guards took us out of our jail cell. I heard the sound of heavy boots—there were seven Russian soldiers, all wearing long military coats, who had been caught by the Germans and were also prisoners in the same jail. Their hands were tied with wires. One of the prisoners, who had a thick black mustache, asked me in Russian, "Ivre?" (Are you Jewish?).

I said "*Da.*"

He answered, "I am also Jewish." I felt a heavy weight lift off my heart. His name was Jacob and he was maybe 21 years old, three years older than me. Jacob told me that he came from Kiev, Russia, and he was a pilot. In Yiddish he said to me, "In case we don't survive, our brothers and sisters will take revenge for us." I will remember this to my dying day. Hearing mamaloushen, the mother tongue of Eastern European Jews, gave me some comfort as we waited for the right or left decision.

The Gestapo took us by truck to the railroad station. Our hands were tied behind our backs with wire. We knew then that we were headed for

Auschwitz. It was July 1944. The guards lifted us up into the cattle car because we could not grab onto the stair rails with our hands. The train was already filled with Polish prisoners who had been captured while trying unsuccessfully to stage an uprising against the Germans in Warsaw.

Once inside the cattle car, if you wanted to stand up you had to ask one of the guards for permission, "Can I stand up? I have to take a leak," and then a prisoner sitting in front of you would open your pants, and the guards would slide the door open a few inches and you'd do your business while the train was still moving.

We were in the cattle car for three or four days, without food, water, or air, sitting in our own filth. We were never let out. The car smelled of urine, feces, and sweat. Throughout the long nights I heard someone crying or yelling out a name or praying for mercy in his sleep. The train moved very slowly, probably because the Germans were trying to save coal. Things were going from bad to worse for the Germans and they no longer saw victory as guaranteed.

One of the Polish prisoners went out of his mind. He stood up without permission and a guard bashed his brains out with the butt of his rifle. His brains landed in my lap and his blood covered my skin. When blood gets cold, it sticks to your skin. I stayed that way for the rest of the journey to Auschwitz with the man's brains and blood on me.

I did not react—my mind was completely numb, empty. I could think of nothing—that is what starvation and torture do to you. I was at the end of the road, without hope. I could not even dream—to have a dream was a luxury and things were happening too fast to hold on to a dream. I felt that this would be the last ride of my life, and I did not care anymore.

The train arrived in Auschwitz, the German name for Oswiecim, a small town about 37 miles west of Krakow. It was as if we were going around in circles with no exit. As I got out of the cattle car with the other prisoners, I heard orchestra music playing for the amusement of the officers. I saw a sign over the gates of the camp, "Arbeit Macht Das Leiben Frei," German for "Work makes you free." We were told to line up and take off our clothes. One of the prisoners who had been in the camp for a few weeks told me, "If you don't survive, you go to the crematorium." He pointed to a smoke stack with black soot spewing from its gaping mouth darkening the sky.

I was handed a black and white striped prison uniform, and then the guards shaved my head. One of the officers asked me my name.

"Josef Kowalski."

I was classified a political prisoner, not a Jew, and handed a red triangle. Jews were given a yellow triangle, and if you were suspected of being a homosexual you were given a purple triangle. Then they tattooed my left arm with the number 189897. I felt like an animal. At that moment, I lost my name and my dignity. I had no identity other than this number burned into my skin. I had no idea what the number meant, but the Nazis had developed an elaborate system to classify prisoners. Some historians have claimed that this system was the brainchild of IBM's collaboration with Germany.

I was assigned to Auschwitz Block 11. Every morning all prisoners had to get up and be counted to make sure that one escaped during the night. The Kapo in charge was a Jew from Lodz named Yosel. I thought that maybe he might have known my family. I whispered to him, "I am David, son of Moshe Chaim Wiener." Before I could say another word, he started beating me up yelling garbage at me. He kicked me right in the groin and then he was finished with me. It didn't matter that we might have known each other in another life. It was as if our past had been eradicated and all that existed was the moment in which we were caught.

In Auschwitz some of the Jews had made a pact with the Devil hoping that somehow their lives would be spared. There were good Jews and bad Jews and Yosel was one of the bad ones. The only humane thing that he did was not to report me as a Jew. I could maintain my status as a political prisoner which in my mind was less dangerous than being classified a Jew.

When the population of a block thinned out due to the death of the inmates, the surviving prisoners would be moved to another block. In short order I was moved from Block 11, to Block 8 and then to Block 5 which was under the supervision of a Polish Communist Kapo, Edy (Edek) who was a gentile from Poznan. By this time my hands were swollen and my belly was sticking out from starvation. I felt faint day and night and was ready to give up on my life. But my friend, Avram Cohen, said, "David, not you. You can't die. We must survive." He gave me the courage to go on. I went to Edy and in Polish I asked him if he would get me a job working in the kitchen. I had to peel potatoes, whatever was needed, and after awhile I started to regain my strength.

One night I was standing outside the barracks. The crematorium was going full blast. After a few minutes, I was covered in black, and the ashes on my lips tasted like bitter snowflakes falling from the sky. A young prisoner came over to me and started speaking German to me. I asked him, "What are you doing here?" Heinz wouldn't answer me. The next night he came over to me again. He told me that he was a lieutenant in the Hitler Youth Movement, the Jugen. His father had been a high-ranking officer in the Vermacht and had been killed in Stalingrad fighting against the Russians. When the Germans found out that Heinz's grandmother was Jewish, they stripped him of his lieutenant's rank and transported him to Auschwitz. In the eyes of the Nazis, he was tainted with Jewish blood and therefore not worth saving.

I then got transferred to Block 4. The Kapo there, who was a political prisoner from Holland, assigned me to the supply room. I was supposed to cut stale loaves of bread into small pieces and dole them out to the prisoners. I used to hide chunks of bread in my groin and bring them back to Block 4 for my fellow prisoners so that they might have a chance to survive. One guy in Block 4 was a tough guy who had been a well-known thief in the underworld of Lodz before the war. His name was Meyer. I used to give him extra bread and in exchange he became my bodyguard. Nobody wanted to mess with me because Meyer was watching my back. Out of desperation, some of the prisoners turned on one another like vultures tearing at the flesh of a dying animal.

One day, a Kapo came into Block 4 and said that the Germans were looking for mechanics to work in the factories around Auschwitz. He told me, "The only way that you are going to get out of here is to say that you are a mechanic."

I asked Granek, another prisoner, who was older than I was, "What do you need to be a mechanic?"

He told me, "Pliers, a file, a few things and you can do the job." Two days later, prisoners were registering for the job of mechanic. It was wintertime and bitter cold, but I thought that I would be better off in a factory job than working in the supply room in Auschwitz and it was the only way that I could get out of there.

There were four or five long tables with German officers sitting behind stacks of papers. While they interrogated us, we had to strip naked so that the officers could inspect our bodies to see if we were sick or starving to death. When I got to the front of the line, the officer asked me, "Are you a *schlosser* (mechanic)?"

"Yes, I am a schlosser, my father was a schlosser and my grandfather was a schlosser. I can do the job. I just need pliers, a file, and a few other tools." I wanted to be sure that they believed me—that I knew what I was doing although, in truth, I hardly had a clue what a mechanic did, but I talked my way into the job.

A couple of days later, the Gestapo took us by train to work at the Messerschmitt factory to build fighter planes for the German army. I felt completely lost. I had never seen the inside of a factory, or an airplane in my entire life. There was a lot of noise from the clatter of airplane parts, rivets, screws, and drilling. I got into the assembly line, and someone handed me a drill which I had no idea how to use. Lucky for me, there was a little Czech prisoner standing next to me who was a real mechanic. "I can see that you are not a mechanic. I'll show you how to use a drill." I followed his example to a point, but I put so much pressure on the drill that I broke it in half and the drill went right into my left thumb. That was my initiation into building an airplane. The factory turned out huge transport gliders, six-engine planes, and the first operational jet fighters, known as the "Swallow."

I worked in the factory for about three or four months. We were supposed to tighten the rivets on the fighter planes but we skipped some of the rivets hoping that there would be an accident when a plane took off or during flight. No one inspected our work or we would have been done for, for sure. None of the prisoners spoke about sabotage, but we all did it.

It was one way that we could contribute to undermining the German war machine.

The Gestapo moved us from the Messerschmitt factory to a camp-site outside Magdeburg, Germany. A railroad cut through the mountains which were over 10,000 feet high. We assembled mechanical parts that were transported along the railroad tracks. The worksite was hidden so deep inside the mountain that when American fighter planes dropped their bombs, we were not even affected by the explosions, and the Allied forces had no idea that we were there. We actually prayed that the bombs would reach us, because we knew if we died the Germans would go down with us. None of the prisoners tried to run away because we were so isolated. There was no place to go.

I used to sleep on the floor at night in the barracks. I did not even have a blanket to keep me from freezing to death. Many of the older prisoners died during the night. When I woke up in the morning there would be a frozen body lying next to me. One of the prisoners working with me was Professor Fogel from Bratislava, Slovakia. He was one of the finest men I ever met. He told me, "David, if you and I survive the war, and you have nobody left in your family, I will adopt you as my son." Soon after he made this pledge to me, he died of starvation. He was only 30 years old and I was 18 or 19. It was painful to get close to anyone because the next day they could be dead, and whatever hope they might have given you with a promise, or a kind gesture, would be annihilated in an instant.

Every morning we were expected to get up and carry the dead bodies and throw them into a ravine. Then we dumped a white powder over the corpses to keep the stench of decaying flesh down and speed up the disintegration of the bodies. I don't even know what I ate to keep my strength up. I tried to keep myself as clean as possible by washing my body in the frozen snow so that my skin would not rot from the dirt that clung to me after working along the railroad tracks. I used to put paper in my shoes to try and keep my feet from freezing. Many of the men suffered from frostbite since we had no socks or winter boots. I felt no emotion; I was like a frozen corpse.

Everyone was dispensable. If you died, there would be someone else waiting in line to take your place. Besides, the Germans were running out of money fighting on two fronts and the last thing that they were thinking about was to make it any easier for us. At one point, one of the German engineers told me that the war was going to come to an end soon. He asked me, "If you survive the war, will you tell the Allies that I was a good German?" He was worried that he would be punished for what he had done during the war and expected me to vouch for him because he gave me an extra piece of bread. I did not answer him.

An announcement was made that we were leaving camp. About 300 men set out from Magdeburg at daylight. If anyone fell behind, the Gestapo shot him. That was it. The Gestapo had police dogs that brought up the end of the line, and I could hear their constant barking urging us to keep moving. This was the beginning of the Death Marches—in my opinion maybe 30 young men in our entire group survived the grueling trek.

Heinz said to me, "Josef, I know this country. Let's stick together." I told him that I did not trust him. He tried to escape; he hardly got 100 yards away from the line before an officer shot him like a dog. If I had followed him, I would have been dead, too. At this point, the Germans wanted to kill as many Jews as possible so that there would be no witnesses to the atrocities that they committed. They knew that once the war ended they were in for it.

We passed through many towns. Kids—maybe 14 or 15 years old wearing the brown uniforms of Hitler's Juden—stood holding rifles almost bigger than they were. We were dying of thirst but they would not let us stop at the fountain in the town square. Instead they started yelling, "Get away, Schweinhund (pig-dog), bloodsuckers, gangsters"—anything to make you feel less than human. I remember when I was working in the barracks at the airport outside the Warsaw ghetto across the Visla River, the Gestapo used to yell, "Schweinhund, drop that shovel. Pick up the manure with your hands." It was a word all too familiar to me. And now the teenagers—infected with the virus of hatred—showed us no mercy, reveling in their power over us.

We marched from town to town along roads lined with ditches where the Germans could run for cover if Allied fighter planes passed overhead, leaving the prisoners out in the open with no escape from the falling bombs. I thought that this was the end for me. Looking back, I can hardly count the number of times that I truly believed my death was imminent.

I told my buddy, Granek, that we should try and escape, "We have nothing to lose." It was now or never. That night the planes started flying over the road where we were marching. The German soldiers made a dash for the ditches leaving us out in the open, as usual. Granek and I found an empty ditch and covered ourselves with a big boulder. The next morning the guards did not notice that we were missing and by a stroke of luck they did not bother to look in the ditch where we were hiding. When we thought they were a safe distance away, Granek and I crawled out of the hole and walked out together. An old man on a bicycle carrying a rifle started yelling at us, "Halt, Halt." With what little strength we had left in us, Granek and I dashed into a shallow stream and the old man was not able to follow us on his bicycle. I remember looking down at the water; it was so clear that you could see the pebbles in the streambed. I was dying to take a drink, but we did not want to risk being caught.

Granek and I walked slowly out in the open as night fell; we could not run because that would have just called attention to us. We tried to blend in although given what we were wearing, and our disheveled and emaciated condition, that thought was probably ludicrous—instead, those Poles who saw us probably made the decision not to chase after us. We weren't worth their trouble.

Granek and I came upon a farm. There was a trough full of food for the pigs. We each stole three potatoes that were black as coal, but they tasted like filet mignon to us—we were starving. There was a hayloft in the barn and we caught a few hours sleep. At daybreak, the farmer spotted us and we started to run to get away from him—we did not know in what direction we were headed. For two nights we slept in an open field. We were actually close to Leipzig, Germany, which was a major target of the Allied forces. In the distance, we heard the sound of falling bombs targeting the city and the sky was intermittently red from firepower. We ate bitter grass growing in the field, but since we did not have a menu, it had to do. At about four o'clock in the morning we saw tanks heading in our direction. It was April 13, 1945.

Granek and I put our hands up. As the tanks came closer, we saw an American flag on the side of the tanks. A heavyset soldier stepped out of one of the cabins and asked us, "Do you speak English?" We answered no.

Another soldier stood up in the tank and yelled out, "Does anyone speak Jewish here?" One of the American soldiers said yes and started speaking to us in broken Yiddish. "Ich bin from Brooklyn, New York" (I am from Brooklyn, New York.)

This was my moment of liberation standing in a field with an American Jewish soldier. I could hardly believe what was happening—that I had endured and survived six years of torture, degradation, homesickness, despair, and sheer emptiness. I had grown from a young boy of 13, to a 19-year old without the joys, the accomplishments, the typical milestones of a normal life that I had dreamed about sitting in my father's lap on the steps of the synagogue on Ul Wolborska, or at the Sabbath table, basking in the love of my parents. All of that was but a dream, a distant memory that I could never recapture. Those days had been stolen from me forever.

An American soldier took Granek and me to the mayor's house in a nearby village. He told him, "Take care of these boys. Feed them. I'll be back to make sure that they are all right." It was clear that if the mayor did not follow our liberator's orders, he would be shot. For the first time in six years, I actually felt safe, that someone was looking out for me, that I no longer needed to count the seconds until a bullet would end my life.

The war in Europe was coming to an end. On April 12, 1945 American soldiers liberated prisoners from Buchenwald, and a few days later Dachau was freed. Soldiers were greeted with the sight of living corpses, men and women staring with vacant eyes, hardly believing that their physical pain and torture were over, although the psychological wounds would follow many of them for the rest of their lives.

On April 15, Vienna fell to the Russians and on April 20, Leipzig was captured by American troops. Ten days later the Russians took control of most of Berlin. Hitler committed suicide on April 30 and on May 7, Germany capitulated to Allied demands and the end of the war in Europe was announced. On May 23, Albert Speer, the German Minister of Economics and Production, responsible for Germany's policy of slave labor, was arrested in his castle. He told the world, "Yes, this is the end. It is a good thing. It was just an opera anyway." The engineer of the Nazi concentration camps, Heinrich Himmler, took the end more seriously. He swallowed a suicide pill rather than face the music.

The nightmare of war ended and my reality began. I asked myself: Who am I? Where am I? Who is left from my family? I had nothing to go back to, no one to show that they cared about me. I could not turn the clock back to the days of my youth that were filled with the love of my parents and brothers and sisters. The Lodz I knew was no more.

For many years after the war, I used to take boiled Spring potatoes and put them in the refrigerator until they turned black as coal on the outside. Then I ate them to remind myself of the potatoes I had stolen from the pigsty to keep myself from starving to death. It took me a long time to break myself of this ritual of remembrance.

chapter four

A MAHOGANY BUREAU

After the Americans handed Granek and me over to the mayor, Russian troops marched into his small town near Leipzig. Russian soldiers had so much hatred for the Nazis that anyone German was considered fair game. They hardly bothered to ask if someone was a Nazi before they blew their brains out. The mayor was lucky that we were staying in his house. We offered him some protection just by being there, and the Russians left him alone. The Russians had a "take no prisoners" attitude.

After some weeks, I had an overwhelming desire to find out if anyone in my family had survived the war. I traveled to Hamburg, Germany which was under the control of the British (all of Germany was being divided up among the Americans, the British, and the Russians). Hamburg had been completed demolished and there was nothing for me there. I traveled to Frankfurt in Main, which was part of the American zone, and stayed in a Displaced Persons (DP) camp for a few days until I found a room in a private house on Rothschild Strasser. An old gentile man and his daughter owned the house. They feared me and treated me well. I was a survivor and in their minds, they were afraid of anyone who could report their behavior to the American occupation forces.

If a Jewish survivor was looking for a place to stay before going to Palestine or to Crete (where Jews were allowed to emigrate under certain circumstances) I offered to share my room with them. I had no money, but at that time, everything was on the barter system since the German mark was worthless. I used to go to the DP camp every few days to check the list of people looking for their relatives who might have survived the war. "David Wiener of Lodz looking for Moshe Chaim Wiener, Hannah Wiener" and so on. Nobody from my family was on the list, but I had not given up all hope, yet. As time passed, it began to dawn on me that no one from my family in Lodz had survived. I eventually learned of their fate from first-hand knowledge, and years later I received an official Deportation Report in Israel listing those in the Lodz ghetto by name, age, and occupation and their age and date of death. Most of my family members were on that list confirming what I knew and what I suspected.

I had a feeling deep inside my heart that the old man and his daughter who owned the house where I was staying were somehow connected to the Nazis. One day, when they were at the market, I snuck into the daughter's bedroom and opened her bureau drawer. It was a beautiful piece of mahogany furniture, and right there—inside the drawer—was the name of a furniture company in Krakow, Poland. I thought surely they must have grabbed it from a Jewish family. (In a recently published book, the author estimated that the gold, stock and bonds, real estate, savings accounts, furnishing, paintings and jewelry looted from murdered Jews accounted for about five percent of the German Reich's operational revenues during the war, and this five percent was often the essential piece that stabilized the vulnerable economies of occupied nations, and guaranteed the Germans comfort back home through bribery and the sale of luxury items at below market prices.)

This plunder also made the difference in how the Nazis were able to successfully turn their country into a people willing to throw the Jews and other minorities to the dogs over and over again.

When the daughter came home I confronted her, "Where is your husband?"

"He is dead. He was a soldier in the German army and he was killed in Stalingrad."

I did not buy her story. I kept on pushing her until she started to cry. She admitted that her husband was an Ober Fuhrer assigned to the Warsaw ghetto. My blood started to boil. "Where is your husband now?"

"I don't know." I hit her a few times and she confessed that her husband was living with his parents outside Frankfurt. She told me that she never really loved her husband because he used to beat her, and she gave me the address where he was staying.

Three of my buddies who were living at the Displaced Persons Camp and I took her father's Opel car and a gun and drove out to the house. His parents opened the door. I asked, "Where is your son?"

"He is not here." When they knew that we meant business they told us that he was coming home from work on the four o'clock train. We waited. Finally, the door opened and I was face to face with the enemy, but for the first time in six years, I had the upper hand.

"Were you SS?" When he answered no, I told him to take his shirt off and I saw the SS tattoo on his arm. I said, "Go down on your knees, Schweinhund and kiss our feet." Then we started beating him. We kicked him in the belly and knocked his kidneys out. I had no pity for him, and all the time that we were beating him up we made his parents watch. I am not proud of what we did, but it felt good to inflict pain upon him. While I was beating him, I kept thinking of how many innocent children and adults he must have murdered. In those moments, he was the embodiment of all that had been done to me and to the millions of prisoners who had been tortured and killed.

It seemed worse to let him live with the pain for the rest of his life. When we got finished with him, he just lay on the floor in his own blood while his parents sobbed at the sight of their son. How many others took revenge I do not know, but I am sure that many who survived the camps were driven to temporary insanity.

The American authorities were looking for me. I had taken the law into my own hands, but I was never punished for what I had done. In fact, I was asked to provide information about Ober Fuhrer Willi Ochs on December 12, 1945. I told the American authorities:

> He was one of the leading men in the ghetto of Warsaw, who had the job of screening the Jews to be sent into jail, concentration camps or who had to be killed. He was a well-known person

in Krakow and Theresienstadt, too. He boasted before his wife and other people of having killed many Jews.

One of my buddies asked me to go back with him to Poland to look for our families. I found out a few weeks later that he had been killed in Kielc. Even after the war had ended, the Poles continued to murder any Jews who might give incriminating evidence to the Allies. The Poles were intent upon wiping out the last of the Jewish population, but they did not entirely succeed. Of the 3,000,000 Jews in Poland before the war, there were approximately 300,000 who survived the war. Today there may be 1,000 Jews living in Poland which once had the largest population of Jews of any country in Europe.

I wanted to get out of Germany. I registered as a schlosser (which meant that I had a trade) with the Hebrew Immigrant Aid Society (HIAS), an American organization that assisted survivors to find safe haven in the United States. As a young person, I had a good chance of getting the help I needed. By that time, I had given up all hope of finding any members of my immediate family.

But something unbelievable happened. My oldest brother, Jacob, had survived the war and was on a train traveling through Italy on his way to Palestine. While he was waiting at the railroad station, he asked some passengers from Lodz if they knew of a Dufce Wiener. "Yes, he is alive and he is living in Frankfurt/Main." Jacob jumped on a train heading back to Frankfurt and in three days he was standing in front of me. That was in July 1946. We had not seen one another since 1939 and could not have imagined that we would ever see one another again. It was truly a miracle, if you believe in miracles. I thought that I was seeing a ghost. We hugged and kissed one another, tears streaming down our faces—I could not tell where his tears ended and mine began.

Jacob had been conscripted into the Polish army at the age of 28; when the Polish army surrendered to the Germans he was thrown into a prisoner-of-war camp. Somehow, he got out and returned to Lodz to warn my mother and father that things were not safe and it was only a matter of time before something terrible was going to happen at the hands of the

Germans. He, together with my brothers Szyje and Yidel went back to Bialystok, Russia, planning to return, but the borders closed at the end of 1940 and the Germans officially declared war on Russia in July 1941 after a brief period of cooperation.

Jacob told me that my brothers had hidden together in a basement. German soldiers killed Szyje on the spot; Yidel escaped deep into Russia and enlisted in the army. He was killed in Stalingrad fighting against the Germans. Jacob escaped but was recaptured by the Germans and sent to Auschwitz. We realized that we were in Auschwitz at the same time. He was working as a carpenter. He lost a finger, but he never talked about what happened to him there. We eventually learned from the German Deportation records that my father died in Lodz in July 1941 at the age of 56; a year later, my mother, my sister, Malka and her husband, and my brother Mendel, also perished along with Jacob's wife, Irene. The Germans liquidated the ghetto in 1944 with most of its population decimated by starvation, disease, or transport to extermination camps.

HIAS gave first priority to the younger displaced persons. I was given a passport and papers to travel to the United States. My passport read "person without a country." My brother Jacob—who was 37 years old—had to wait for his emigration papers, but he too eventually came to America.

chapter five

BEWARE OF PITY

I boarded the S.S. General Black, an American military ship that had been converted into a passenger transport after the war. There were over 1,000 passengers on board with many young children, traveling alone because they had lost their parents. To accommodate everyone, the dormitory where I slept had row after row of bunk beds. The crossing was so rough that the ship almost sank. Despite the storms I did not get sick.

I hooked up with Nathan Mlynarksy, a Jewish guy from Poland, and three other fellows who were about the same age as me—19 or 20. We all stuck together, but we did not speak very much about what had happened to us during the war. I was still totally numb. Hate and bitterness overwhelmed me, which was perhaps a protection against feeling the unbearable sadness of knowing that almost my entire family, save my brother Jacob, had been lost. I could not grasp the thought that I would never again see my brothers and sister, and my mother and father. I suppressed any emotions that might have been just below the surface. I think that everyone was "in the same boat" so to speak. Sometimes, I felt that I was living in a strange dream on that boat, just heading toward an uncertain future in America, but away from the blood of Europe that had washed over me for almost six years. I could only focus on the present.

When the ship entered the New York harbor I distinctly remember seeing the Statue of Liberty but I did not truly know what she stood for—freedom and a welcoming hand—things that I scarcely knew the meaning of. Representatives of the Hebrew Immigration Aid Society were waiting for us as we disembarked the ship. They took us right away to the Marseilles Hotel on 103rd Street and Broadway, on Manhattan's west-side. I went back there three years ago, and it has been converted into a home for old people, but in 1946, it was a way station for Jewish refugees like Nathan Mlynarsky and me.

HIAS was responsible for finding a permanent place for us to live and those young people under their supervision were sent to different cities around the United States. After some time in Manhattan, Nathan and I were sent to the East Liberty section of Pittsburgh, Pennsylvania. East Liberty was predominantly a Jewish neighborhood. We stayed with a wonderful family who gave us a room in their attic. They had a heart of gold and they understood our pain. Two brothers in the family ran a delicatessen. HIAS then found me a job working for two old men who owned Wolk Brothers, a wholesale clothing company. They paid me 75 cents an hour cleaning the floor, packing the goods for shipment. Every day at about noon, I used to go to a fast-food restaurant. I'd sit at the counter and the waitress wouldn't charge me anything for the food. I didn't speak English, but somehow we communicated. She was really generous.

Jack Wolk used to give me a few extra dollars to help me out. He told me not to tell anyone. I started going to night school to learn English. This was the first time since I had been in Krotoszyn, Poland, living with my brother, Jacob, and his wife, Irene, that I was back in a classroom. The war had put an abrupt end to my studies, and my dream of some day becoming a lawyer, was destroyed in the camps along with everything else in my life. But I was determined to learn English as fast as I could because I knew that that was my ticket to a better job. I also studied American history. The teacher helped me out because she could see that I was an earnest student. She was a beautiful person.

After awhile I moved to a room on Philips Avenue in Square Hills, a better neighborhood, while I was still worked for Wolk Brothers. Every night I had dinner at A.S. Delicatessen on Foothill Boulevard. (This address would hold special significance for me later in my life.) I ordered the same thing at every meal: eggs and salami, which tasted better than any steak or lobster that I have eaten since. I met some people in the delicatessen who told me that there was a customer who was from Lodz. I was curious who the guy was. They told me that he sold clothing and bedding around Pittsburgh.

I wanted to meet him. He was a short, little fellow. He asked me, "Where do you come from? I told him," I come from Lodz. I am the son of Moshe Chaim Wiener."

"Did he study with the Gerer Rebbe, Abraham Mordecai Alter, and teach at the synagogue on Wolborska Street?" I said yes. He started crying like a baby. He wanted to invite me to his house for Shabbat dinner, but I was reluctant to go because I felt that he was inviting me out of feelings of pity. Eventually, I accepted his invitation but I barely ate anything. I didn't want to show them how hungry I really was for a home-cooked meal—it was false pride.

He asked me if I would like to come to his warehouse where he had a huge inventory for the peddlers that worked the streets in and around Pittsburgh. Many of the peddlers sold goods to the coal miners in small towns like Arlington. He bought Nate and me a car—an old Plymouth— so that we could cover a large enough territory to make some money. I already had learned how to drive a car while I was in Germany, so I got my license without much trouble. Nate and I formed our own business, and this guy was our supplier. We loaded up the car with bed sheets, dresses, bathrobes, silverware, and all kinds of items for the house including pots and pans. We took everything on consignment. Once we sold the goods, we split the proceeds with our supplier. Most of our clients were Polish gentiles and I used to speak to them in Polish and in English. I wanted them to know that I was Polish.

Sometimes, I'd see women the same age as my mother or my sister, walking on the street in the better neighborhoods, dressed nicely, with their hair styled, and their red nail polish and I had a hard time accepting the injustice of it all. I tried to push these thoughts from my mind.

Nate and I worked five days a week and on the weekends we would sometimes take in a movie, whatever happened to be playing at our local movie theater. I never went to synagogue except on the High Holy Days. I really believed that God had let us down. How could he have abandoned Jews like my parents who were so devout, who believed in the God Almighty?

Truthfully, my father worshipped God with blind faith adhering to the strictest tenets of Orthodox Judaism. One time I went to a mikvah with him and I noticed that one of his toes was missing. I asked my brother Szyje what had happened to my father. He told me, "Father did not want to go into the army during World War I so he cut off his own toe so that he would be ineligible. He couldn't bear the thought of eating non-kosher food. He saw it as a sacrilege against God." Later he starved to death in the ghetto rather than eat traif; unkosher food.

I am sorry that I cannot understand his orthodoxy, but it is one of the reasons that I am unable to hold God in my heart. This is not to say that I am not proud to be a Jew and I have tried to instill that pride in my children, Helene and Michael. I want them to know where they came from and who they are. On the one hand there is the question of the existence of God, and on the other hand there is the undeniable knowledge and proof of your Jewish roots. And perhaps most important of all is the knowledge that the Jews are a strong people, that in spite of everything we have survived and that the Nazis could not completely wipe us out. That is my faith, my belief, and it has nothing to do with going to a synagogue or keeping kosher. You might say that I am a secular Jew in my heart.

Nate and I were doing pretty well. He worked one side of the street and I worked the other going door-to-door selling whatever goods we had picked up on consignment. One day, Nathan knocked on somebody's door. The lady yelled out, "Not today, not today." Nathan was astonished and he told me, "I wonder how she knew my name. He thought she said, "Nathan, go." His English was not very good, and when I explained what she had said we had a good laugh.

There were a lot of people in Pittsburgh who did not know anything about what had happened to us during the war. They really did not want to hear what we had been through, or if they heard stories about the Holocaust they really did not believe much of what they heard. The local newspapers barely carried any information. Even The New York Times, which was owned by Jews, downplayed the reports of Nazi atrocities and so it was not surprising that people were so ignorant.

One day I was having lunch at A.S. Delicatessen. One of the customers asked me, "How did you survive the war? What did you go through?" I didn't say much. A Jewish butcher said, "We had a tough life here in America, too. We had to wait in line for sugar and meat during the war." I looked at him with pity because he was so ignorant. Why didn't he know about the torture and starvation that the Jewish people endured during the war? Waiting in line for rations seemed a benign sacrifice for your country compared to what the Jews of Eastern Europe had been subjected to. But it was not an argument that I chose to start.

HIAS visited us and asked how Nate and I were doing. I told them, "I like America." They asked me what my ambitions were before the war. They offered to send me back to school so that I could eventually become a lawyer, but I would not accept what I saw as a handout. It was a matter of pride. I told them, "I can do it on my own." Had things been different, my older brothers would have helped to put me through law school in Poland since early in my schooling I had ranked very high on intelligence tests and had done well in school until tenth grade when I could no longer go to school. We were a very close-knit family and whatever one person needed, everyone else pitched in to provide it. There was no such thing as a handout, and loyalty to family was paramount.

Nate and I went back to New York City in late 1947. We split up and I lived in a rooming house on 97th Street between Broadway and Amsterdam Avenues on the westside. At night, cockroaches crawled up the wall of my room. During the day they hid in the walls or under my bed, avoiding the daylight. The renters in the hotel were garment cutters, taxi cab drivers, restaurant workers. I used to go back to the Marseilles Hotel to see if any of my buddies was still there. A good-looking kid was playing pool next to the lobby. I watched him for awhile. "David, why don't you play with me? I'll teach you the tricks. You can make good money at pool." I resented his offer. I told him, "It's not my cup of tea." I stopped going to the hotel because it had started to attract a gang element and I did not want to be a part of that. I also could not do anything that would have been shameful

in my parents' eyes or hurt them in any way. I wanted to live by their standards of goodness and righteousness.

And then I received a postcard from a friend who had gone to Los
Angeles. I don't know how Martin even knew where I was living unless
he had contacted HIAS and they had given him my address. Somehow, I
scraped the money together for an airplane ticket to Los Angeles without
any assurances that things would be better, except that Martin told me he
had a job working for an upholster and that life was pretty good in Los
Angeles.

chapter six

THE GIRL WITH DARK HAIR AND BEAUTIFUL BLUE EYES

I saw a "for rent" sign in the window of a house in Los Angeles' Fairfax district at 427 North Curson Street off Beverly Boulevard. The family who owned the house were Jews from Canada. I moved in with them for a short time. They had a daughter who was very beautiful and they kept pressing me to go out with her, but I was emotionally frozen and I had no capacity for giving love to anyone, no matter how special or how beautiful she might be.

The only way that I could get out of this awkward situation gracefully was to move. I found a room in a house nearby, owned by the Richmond family nearby at 171 South Gardner Avenue. I shared a room with a French Jewish guy named Bob. Two girls from Chicago lived in another room in the house which made it a very busy place. I didn't have a chance to feel lonely with all the comings and goings of my housemates. I got a job working in the Richmond's big laundry downtown on Main Street that serviced the hotels in the city. It was hot, hard work hauling the heavy sheets and towels, but it paid the bills. After a few weeks I quit that job—I did not see any future in it and it was not challenging.

I got a job selling Deluxe vacuum cleaners door-to-door in Santa Monica, which was a good territory because there were many families of different nationalities moving into the neighborhood after the war. The city was really booming and vacuum cleaners were an important item for new homeowners and renters. Usually, I was guaranteed a sale if I had the chance to demonstrate how the vacuum cleaner worked. I used to say, "Vacuum cleaners are good for your health, and it is much more convenient than a carpet sweeper or a broom." I did pretty well since I had a knack as a salesman; I was a hard worker and I had the determination to succeed.

On Friday and Saturday evenings, I used to go out with other Holocaust survivors to a dance hall on Western Avenue and Sixth Street across town. There was a live band, and after a few drinks I was a pretty good talker, but I had no desire or motivation to take anyone out although there were many available attractive girls there who liked to dance with me. Those evenings were something I could look forward to after a hard week selling vacuum cleaners door-to-door.

Then I started selling jewelry and silverware in Boyle Heights in East Los Angeles from a supplier on Highland Avenue who only sold to peddlers. Boyle Heights was a very mixed neighborhood. Latino and Jewish families lived side by side and the talk on the street was Yiddish, Spanish, and English. The main attraction of the area was the Breed Street Shul. Years later the shul was abandoned as Jewish families moved away. Until recently pigeons and mice occupied the pews, but there are plans to turn the shul into a community center for the remaining Latino families, and what was once Brooklyn Avenue is now named after the famous Latino farm workers' organizer, Caesar Chavez.

I was guaranteed so much a week selling door-to-door and I guess I did pretty well because I could afford to buy myself a car—an old 1941 Chevrolet—which got me around. But I quit that job too and in 1950 I took a sales job working door-to-door for Covington Upholstery. I made $50 a week plus commission, which did not keep me satisfied for very long, and I realized that I needed to learn a trade, not just keep selling without a guaranteed income or a real future.

I took a job working for Dawson Upholstery which was owned by two Jewish brothers. They taught me how to take furniture apart and make cushions. At the same time, I enrolled in a night class at Fairfax High School to improve my English. During a break, I saw a skinny, pretty girl with dark hair and beautiful, blue eyes leaning against the door to our classroom. I asked her, "Do you speak Yiddish?

"A little bit." Renée Freilich was from Brussels, Belgium. She had also survived the war and had recently come to Los Angeles. I took her out on a couple of dates. I felt very comfortable with her because she instinctively understood my pain; I did not have to say very much and yet we were able to communicate. American girls could not even begin to understand what I had gone through and I could not have a conversation with them. We really had no common ground.

Renée lived in a little room with a kitchenette in the 1400 block of Poinsettia Avenue. She invited me to breakfast. I began to feel like a human being again. I can say that Renée and I were like two leaves without a branch that had been blown by the winds of war from place to place. We felt rootless, but together we felted connected to one another, and soon we started going steady.

Renée was working for the Plasma Laboratory on Sunset Boulevard near Alvarado Street downtown. Her job was to separate the plasma from the blood. Slowly she told me some of the details of her life as if she were letting me read one page at a time of a private diary only meant for her. At a young age, her parents left her in a hospital outside Antwerp, Belgium and when the war broke out, there was not enough food for the patients and the aides and she had to fend for herself. She nearly starved to death. She escaped Belgium into Switzerland in a truck hiding under the hay with other young people. The roads were icy and the truck driver lost control, and the truck overturned spilling out its precious human cargo. Somehow, Renée survived and ended up in the United States. Unfortunately, her father and a sister and brother-in-law were all murdered in Auschwitz. Her mother left Belgium and ended up in Poland before the war but she also perished.

Renée went to Chicago where her Uncles Joe, Aaron and Al had settled before the war broke out in Europe. She lived with her uncle Al for a short time, but his family—especially her cousin—was embarrassed by her European refugee ways and her accent and did not welcome her with open arms. To add to her troubles, Al's wife was jealous of Renée, and did not want her husband to share his attention among the three women in his house. She treated Renée as less than a "second class citizen" and the situation proved intolerable. Renée made up her mind to leave. She followed her only friend, Gabby, to Los Angeles. She used to tell me, "The only thing that I own is my body." She was free to go wherever she wanted, and it was our good fortune that fate brought us together at a class to learn English.

One night I took Renée out to dinner at a nice Czech restaurant on Sunset Boulevard near Spaulding Avenue. I wanted to impress her. Renée told me, "Don't spend money on me, David." And that is how she always was. After what she had endured, human companionship and devotion were far more important to her than material possessions or the luxury of an expensive meal that might have "eaten up" an entire week's paycheck.

And then in 1951, we received some unexpected news. I got a letter from the United States government telling me that I was eligible for the army. Although I was not yet a naturalized citizen, the country was at war with Korea, and the army was on an aggressive recruitment campaign. I did not expect to be called up, but I had no choice. I went down to the Army Recruitment office on Figueroa Street. The officials checked me out and said I was healthy enough to serve. I got my orders to report to Fort Ord on the Monterrey Peninsula just south of San Francisco. It is considered the most beautiful army base in the United States, and not a bad place to spend a weekend, but I certainly did not want to serve in the army after everything that I had been through. In fact, I was surprised that the army was even willing to accept me with the injuries that I had suffered during the war, and how much my health had been compromised by living in a constant state of starvation and physical and psychological torture.

Renée and I said our goodbyes and I boarded a bus heading to Ford Ord along with other Army recruits. I couldn't believe that I was back in an army barracks, albeit under very different circumstances. I somehow felt betrayed and I was determined to get through my tour of duty without being killed. I did not want to end up an anonymous casualty of the Korean War with no one to pray for me or cry for me if I did not survive combat.

When Renée had enough time off from her job to make the trip, she would drive my Chevrolet up the coast with other friends to visit me. We took long walks around the camp because I was not eligible for a pass to leave Fort Ord. I don't remember that we spoke of our future together, but I am sure that it was on our minds, although there was the threat of combat duty hanging over my head.

When Renée was not able to visit me, my Catholic army buddy, Tony, and I went to synagogue on Saturdays and on Sundays we'd go to church since it gave us something to do and a way to avoid kitchen duty.

We had a very tough sergeant who gave us the news that we were heading for Korea. I told the sergeant, "I want to see the doctor."

He barked at me, "What for?"

"I don't feel good. I have headaches." The lieutenant sent me to Dr. Levine who had served in Germany with the United States Army during World War II. He saw the numbers burned under my arm and recognized that I was a Holocaust survivor. He looked at me and said, "You have been through enough. I am going to put you in the hospital." But Captain Kelly, the head of my platoon threatened me, "If you don't want to go to Korea, why we'll just send you back to Poland where you came from." He initiated court-martial proceedings, but Dr. Levine argued my case and it was dismissed. I received an honorable discharge from the army on May 19, 1951 just 11 days before my 25th birthday, three months after my induction into the army. Another angel must have been standing on my shoulder.

My brother, Jacob, followed me to the United States, although he had to wait for some time for all his papers to be put in order. Age was not on his side which accounted for the delay in his departure. He rented an apartment on Atlantic Avenue in Brooklyn and opened a shoe store on

125th Street and Amsterdam Avenue in Harlem where he used to buy closeout shoes and rejects which he would fix up for resale. I stayed with him after I was discharged from the Army and he offered me a job working in his store to tide me over until something better came along. Renée planned to join me in New York after making a stop in Chicago for a cousin's wedding.

Jacob was a very bitter and disappointed man; he never recovered from the loss of his wife, Irene, and he did not have the comfort of children to give him some hope in the future. Besides, he hated what he was doing; he had had a beautiful family life with luxuries in Krotoszyn and now he was reduced to menial tasks that brought him very little money or prestige. He started gambling on horses and his days were often spent at the racetrack. Truthfully, he was a living casualty of the war.

I believe that age is a big factor in a human being's ability to recover. Adults who had a full life before the war had a much harder time picking up the pieces of their lives than those younger victims whose lives were not well defined. The older survivors did not have the resilience of youth on their side. Despite his own disappointments in later years, Jacob was very proud of me. He used to introduce me to all his friends as his successful younger brother.

The Old Market Square, Lodz, Poland, with the "Alshtot" Synagogue at UI Wolborska (1916).

My father's mother and father in Lublin (1918).

I have no pictures of my parents.

Orthodox Jews leaving the synagogue. The apartment where I lived as a child was on the seventh floor of the building just to the left of the synagogue (1937).

In Krotoszyn, 1939. Back row: three Polish Jewish soldiers stationed near the town with a young woman who owned one of the town's bakeries; front row: I am standing next to my brother, Jacob, and to his right is another Polish Jewish soldier.

My Aunt Pearl Gilbert, my mother's sister, with her family: her daughter, Rachel Lerner and her husband, Szyre Lerner with their three children. Only Szyre and his oldest child survived the Holocaust.

Standing in front of a memorial at a Displaced Persons (DP) Camp outside Frankfurt in Main, just after World War II.

A rally at the DP Camp. The sign reads, "Freedom can only be with the realization of a Jewish National Home—Palestine."

Left to right: my buddy, Granek, who escaped the Death March with me, Abraham Gilbert (my cousin) and me before I left for America.

Friends in Frankfurt/Main. I am standing on the right (1946).

I kept these black and whitestriped prison pants and put them on to take this picture.

At the new installation of my father's grave.

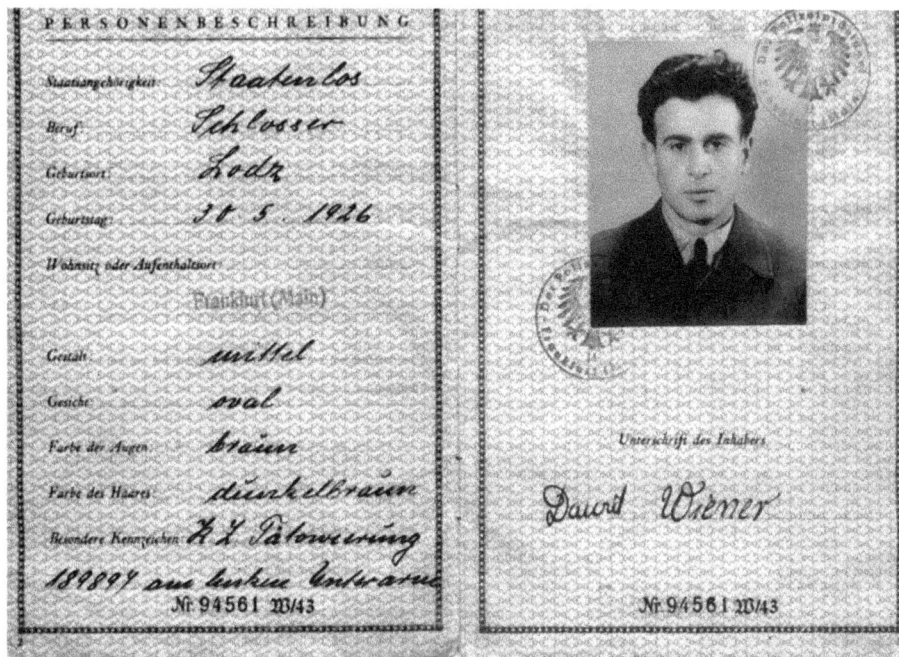

My passport which documented that I was a schlosser and had number 189897 tattooed on my arm.

Shortly after arriving in New York City. I am with three buddies (left to right) Smuleck, a street peddler, David, who killed himself, and a guy who worked as a cab driver.

On Broadway and 98th Street near the Marseilles Hotel, Manhattan (1950).

My brother, Jacob, in Brooklyn (1951).

In Los Angeles under a street sign that reads "Sunset Boulevard" (1950).

In my army uniform at Ford Ord, California (1951).

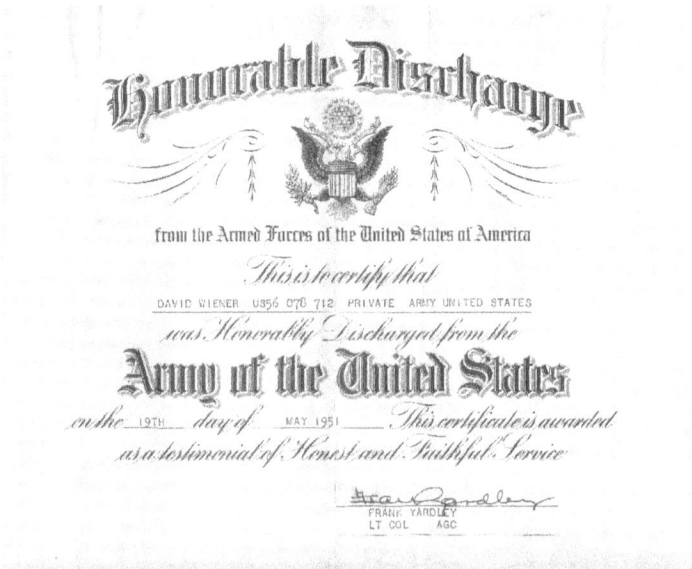

My Honorable Discharge Certificate from the Armed Forces of the Unites States of America, May 1951.

During the summer of 1951, I took a job as an assistant cook at the Alpine Hotel in the Catskill Mountains, where many Jewish middle class families spent their vacations. The area was known as the "Borscht Belt" and it was a place where Jewish comics like Jackie Mason, Mel Brooks, and Shecky Greene got their start. On the weekends Renée and Jacob would drive up to the Alpine Hotel to visit me. When Renée saw me plucking chicken feathers and boiling eggs in the hotel kitchen she nearly fainted. I don't think that she had ever seen me working like that before.

After the dining room was cleared of guests, Renée and I would sit outside breathing the fresh mountain air, and look up at the moon and stars which were so clear because there were no city lights to interfere with their brilliance. We talked late into the night. Some of the guys played baseball on the lawn and we used to watch their games. We stayed in a bungalow reserved for the help in the back of the hotel. Our quarters weren't very luxurious, but we had our privacy. Sometimes I would wake up in the middle of the night screaming and sweating from a horrible nightmare, and Renée would comfort me. Those nightmares sometimes still visit me to this day.

After the summer was over, I went back to work for my brother in his shoe store. I did not like the neighborhood, the clientele, or the business so I quit.

I had a black Chevrolet panel truck and I would load up the truck with dolls to sell at Christmastime at a big swap meet in Lodi, New Jersey. I bought the inventory myself and did pretty well. I met a Jewish guy there named Ronnie who came from Philadelphia. His parents were wealthy and he was spoiled. I don't think that he had ever seen anyone work as hard as I did. He took a liking to me and said, "David, let's go into business together." We decided to go into the soap business—we used to put Fink Detergent into big containers and sell them to customers at the swap meet. The product slogan was, "Fink Detergent cleans carpets. Guaranteed!" To generate sales, we demonstrated how our detergent removed carpet stains. One of our customers came over to our stall and started shouting, "Get that son-of-a-bitch. That soap doesn't work." I yelled to Ronnie, "Run, run." We left everything behind in our stall. The guy was a real thug; he was wearing denim overalls and had the body language of a long shoreman; I don't think that Ronnie and I would have won a fight against him.

Ronnie left the business—it was too tough for him. I switched to selling bananas. It was safer. I used to pick up half-ripe bananas from a produce distributor at four o'clock in the morning and set up my stall. By noon, with the sun beating down on the bananas, they were pretty ripe, and I managed to make $50 a day. While I was working in Lodi, New Jersey, Renée, who was living with a cousin, got a job in a garment factory making ladies' silk lingerie. She was an excellent seamstress.

One of Renée's cousins, Bernie Goldwasser, who was in the garment business, came to speak to me about my intentions toward Renée. He didn't beat around the bush, "Why don't you and Renée settle down?" I was tired and I did not want to lose Renée. Besides I did not have the luxury of being a romantic at the time so I just answered, "Fine." My matterof-fact answer to him hid a deep well of emotions that over time I uncovered to Renée. Slowly, I regained my ability to feel and to love after so many years of just surviving—living like a person with a frozen heart just going from day to day not knowing if I might be taking my last breathe. It was hard to become attached to anyone after all that I had lost. I don't even think that I told Renée that I loved her but I did ask her to marry me and she accepted. I think that she intuitively understood what was in my heart even if I could not yet express my feelings to her.

Renée had another cousin, Schneier, who lived in Brooklyn. She offered to make us an Orthodox Jewish wedding. I bought a drapery ring for two cents from Woolworth's Department Store which was all that I could afford for our ceremony which took place on October 7, 1951. In the Jewish tradition, we wrapped ourselves in a tallis, a shawl with fringes, to symbolize the union of marriage. There were 15 guests—mostly relatives—at our wedding and we served wine and cookies. The entire wedding probably cost $50. Afterwards, Renée and I spent our wedding night at the Times Square Hotel in Manhattan. It wasn't very romantic, because there was a house of prostitution right next door, and we could hear the customers running up and down the stairs, but it did not matter to us.

We moved into a two-room apartment in the Williamsburg section of Brooklyn on 111 South Third Street. The apartment was owned by one of Renée's cousins and we paid $45 a month in rent. On November 6, 1952 I became a naturalized citizen. This was a big accomplishment for me because I had to learn to read and write in English well enough to pass the citizenship test. I believed that it was a necessary step toward getting ahead in America; Renee became a naturalized citizen in 1956.

Renée quit her job in the lingerie factory and became my right hand working at the swap meet in Lodi. We started selling tomatoes as well as bananas. I had the idea of putting tomatoes in little cartons and wrapping them up in cellophane. I was able to sell them for three times the price that I would have gotten if I had sold each tomato individually. They were an instant hit, because they encouraged people to buy more than one tomato at a time, they were easy to carry, and the packaging protected the tomatoes from bruising. I realized that presentation was an important part of marketing. We were doing really well although the work was backbreaking and we were on our feet all day. But we were free and no one was chasing us or calling us Zydek, dirty Jew.

On Sundays, we used to catch a show at Radio City Music Hall near 51st Street in Manhattan. I was standing outside the theater and Karl Frankel, a guy that I knew from Los Angeles, came up to me. "David, what are you doing here?"

"My wife and I are seeing a show." I told him I was working at a swap meet selling produce. He said, "Let's go back to California." Renée did not really like living in New York; it was too big for her, so without a moment's hesitation, we loaded up our black, panel truck with everything that we owned, which wasn't much, and drove across the country. We were like two turtles carrying our home on our backs. Renée's motto, "The only thing I own is my body," was now true for both of us. We were unencumbered and could take a chance at a new life. It was March 1952 and we drove ten hours a day for almost six days, stopping briefly in Chicago to visit Renée's Aunt Sally and Uncle Aaron.

On our way driving through the mountains of Arizona, the truck barely made it, jerking and puttering along. I'd step on the gas to make it up a steep incline and the truck would move just a few feet before slowing down. It kept overheating so we had to stop to cool the engine down every few hundred miles, sometimes in the hot desert, sometimes on a busy highway. Somehow the truck did not break down and we slowly made it all the way to Los Angeles. We rented a little apartment at 412 South Rampart Boulevard near Alvarado Street in the low-rent district. I was starting over again, but this time I had a loving partner who was behind me in everything that I did. Eventually, my brother, Jacob, followed us to Los Angeles.

chapter seven

BUILDING A BUSINESS
IS LIKE MAKING CHALLAH

The weather was particularly warm in Los Angeles our first summer in the city, and our apartment had no air conditioning. Even when the sun went down, it was stifling in our apartment because we had no cross ventilation. Renée and I decided to go to a local movie theater on Alvarado and Wilshire Boulevard. We did not care what was playing, but the theater was air-conditioned and that was really all that we wanted—a break from the heat. When we got to the box office window, I reached into my pocket and discovered that I only had 98 cents, 2 cents less than what we needed for tickets. The manager would not let us in and we had to go back to our little "hotbox" of an apartment. This incident sticks in my mind, to this day.

I went back to work selling upholstery door-to-door. I had lots of gimmicks, "Special today, no charge, no obligation." I made the usual $50 a week plus commission by following up on customer leads. Renée got a job sewing for an upholsterer. By that time, I knew that I would go into the upholstery business myself. I thought, "If I can do it for them, I can do it for myself."

What I lacked in experience I made up for in sheer guts. I went back to my old employer, Dawson Upholstery, and they gave me a cushion machine, some supplies, and I leased a heavy-duty sewing machine. I opened Cosmos Upholstery at 5174 Melrose Avenue. Renée worked in the shop, sewing and answering the telephone as leads came in. I used to drive to Long Beach Boulevard near Alameda Street and to Compton. Most of the people living in that area were named Washington, Jefferson, Madison, and Adams—African Americans who had taken the names of presidents. It was a real blue-collar neighborhood and there was very little competition from other Los Angeles upholsterers who did not want to bother traveling the distance or go into unfamiliar neighborhoods. I thought, "I am going to go where the business is." I used to offer "a special sale today, half off."

I remember one of my first house calls. The lady asked me, "What color goes with green?" I didn't know colors from borscht and Renée gave me some tips. Our first sale was reupholstering a sofa bed. I was anxious to succeed and I was sincere with my customers. I felt like a million dollars when I made my first sale. After awhile I hired two ladies to help me work the territory. They would take one side of the street and I would take the other.

Usually, I closed three out of five leads. I was a pretty good salesman. But I remember one day, I had no leads at all, and I was coming up completely empty going door-to-door and it was already turning dark out. But I did not want to go home until I made a sale. I saw a light on in a house and I knocked on the door. A policeman answered. I said, "Good evening, sir, could you use any upholstery? We have a special sale today."

He told me to come in and invited me to have dinner with his family. He asked me where I was from and before I knew it he said, "Well, I have a sofa that needs fixing." After dinner, we loaded the sofa into my black, panel truck and I had made a sale at seven o'clock in the evening. That incident taught me a good lesson—never give up. Determination pays off in the end.

Now that I was beginning to build up a solid clientele, I had another problem. People wanted to pay for work over time on credit—they needed a loan for a year or 18 months, but I needed to get paid right away for the work that I did in order to pay my bills and support Renée and me. I had no way to extend my customers credit because I had no cash reserves. We were working from sale to sale at that time. Customers were even willing to pay up to 18 percent interest in order to pay over time, but every loan company that I contacted who specialized in high interest rate paper, turned me down.

I had almost given up looking, when I spotted a loan company on the corner of Wilshire Boulevard and La Jolla Avenue near the Fairfax district, which is predominantly a Jewish neighborhood. I walked in the door and told the receptionist that I wanted to see the boss. She said, "He's not in yet," but I could see him through a glass partition sitting in his office at the end of the hall. I walked down the hall and stood in front of his desk which was neat as a pin. He was a young, skinny guy. Surprised that I was in his office, he looked at me and said, "Who are you? Do you have an appointment with me?"

"No, and never mind who I am. I need your help." "What do you need?"

"I am in the upholstery business. I need someone who can buy my receivables so that I can extend credit to my customers." He asked me again, "What is your name?"

This time I answered him. "My name is David Wiener and I own Cosmos Upholstery on Melrose.

He said, "Well, I'll come to your shop and see how you are doing."

I said, "I know you will not come," but he assured me that he would keep his word. I think that I had become so discouraged by this time, that I did not even want to trust my own good luck.

And then he actually showed up at my shop which was dirty and dusty with one light bulb hanging down from the ceiling. He was well-dressed in a blue, pinstriped suit. I dusted off one of the chairs so that his suit would not get dirty. He sat down and started asking me more questions: "Where do you come from? How much do you have in receivables? How much money would you like to make a month?" All the time the phone was ringing, and we looked very busy.

To the last question, I answered, "If I can make five hundred dollars a month, I would be the happiest man in the world." Five hundred dollars was big money to me in those days. I was pacing back and forth which has become one of my habits when I am excited or nervous.

He looked at me and said, "David, please sit down. Were your parents religious Jews?" I did not know where he was going with this line of questioning, but I answered him honestly, "Yes, my parents were very religious. My father was an Orthodox teacher in Lodz, Poland."

"Do you remember on Friday nights how your mother made challah? She started with a small piece of dough. Then she added water and the challah got bigger and bigger. Well, business is like challah. You take care of one customer and then by word of mouth you get another customer and your business will get bigger and bigger." He promised that he would buy customer paper from me. He was a real mensch and he kept his promise. And he was right about my business. It grew like challah.

I always took care of my customers. If anyone complained, I always came back to find out what was wrong. I told my customers, "I will always be there for you." People used to tell me. "Mr. Wiener, no one else is like you. Once we pay someone else, we never see them again. But you always stand by your work."

My business kept expanding and I was able to eliminate the lower-paying jobs. I started going to homes where customers were giving me orders for upholstering better-quality furniture. I had a beautiful clientele—doctors, lawyers, and well-to-do professional people. I stopped making the long drive to Compton and Long Beach Avenue and concentrated on customers in more upscale neighborhoods. I stopped soliciting leads, and I did not have to spend a nickel on advertising. All my jobs came from recommendations of other satisfied customers. It wasn't long before I was making a lot more than $500 a week. I also started making custom furniture on order. I was working ten hours a day, six days a week. Renée worked in the shop until three o'clock in the afternoon, and then she would go home to make dinner for us. Sometimes we went out to eat at a neighborhood restaurant on Melrose Avenue if she was too tired to cook. We worked side by side which made the long hours less difficult and we shared the same desire to succeed.

I had some eccentric and unusual clients. One lady had just moved from New York City to Grammercy Place near Melrose Avenue. I had recovered a sofa for her and I went to her home to deliver it. I asked her, "Where do you want the sofa?"

"Just put it over there?" "Over here?"

"Oh, don't bother me." "Don't you know who is playing?" She was watching a baseball game on television.

"No ma'am, I don't."

"The Dodgers and the Yankees. It's the World Series." Stupidly, I said, "Who are the Dodgers and the Yankees?"

She turned around and said, "You don't know who they are? You must be a dead living person." That was really funny. I was so busy trying to make a living that I did not have time to follow baseball, but I realized that if I wanted to get along with my clients I better learn more about the teams and the World Series. I started asking people about first base, second base, pitching, the teams, batting averages. It was a way to fit in—to be part of this country. And it was something to talk about to customers who liked to chat with me about things other than furniture and upholstery.

Two of my best clients lived in a residential hotel, The Fairfield, on Franklin Avenue: Mrs. Miles was from Chicago (she could trace her family back seven generations and there is a town in Illinois named after her family) and Mrs. McCue. I furnished Mrs. McCue's entire apartment—draperies, furniture, the works. She was about 75-years old and a widow. Her family owned a cement business and she had a full-time chauffeur who used to drive her around town to the symphony and the ballet. She was wealthy and very cultured.

I think that she was lonely because whenever I came by in my black, panel truck to deliver a piece of furniture she used to say, "Sit down, Mr. Wiener."

"Mrs. McCue, have I done something wrong?"

"No, Mr. Wiener I just like talking with you." We might have discussed music, or maybe even baseball since I had learned a thing or two about the World Series by then. I never shared my life story with her. I did not want her pity. I might have told her that I was originally from Poland but that was it. I have always told my children that pity is the worst thing that anyone can have for you.

Mrs. McCue was a lovely lady. One day, she told me that she had gone to a party at her daughter's house. Her daughter's husband was a producer and director in Hollywood and they used to throw lavish parties with a live orchestra playing popular dance tunes. She said, "You know, Mr. Wiener, in my heart I am still young. I want to live, to dance, but my legs won't let me." At the time, I really did not understand what she meant, but as I get older, I have come to appreciate the truth of what she said to me.

Mrs. McCue really embraced life. In contrast, I had another customer who was preoccupied with her own death, in a most unusual way. A little, skinny woman in her seventies came into Cosmos Upholstery. She was very nicely dressed and looked as if she had money. She told me that she lived in the mid-Wilshire district, which was a very affluent part of the city.

She asked me, "Mr. Wiener, do you make coffins?" She figured if I was making furniture, why not a coffin?

"Yes, of course we do." I didn't know the first thing about making coffins, but I never said no to any customer's request so long as it was legal. "Well, I'd like you to make me a coffin to my size. I'd like to have it lined in pink, tufted satin upholstery with a soft pillow for my head." I measured her and she left me a deposit for half the cost. I called a carpenter, and he brought a custom-made coffin in mahogany to the workshop. We fitted the coffin with the upholstery that she picked out and I called her to tell her that her coffin was ready.

She climbed into the coffin and closed her eyes. "Ah, it is so comfortable. I am very happy. Please ship it to the mortuary. They will take care of it." She paid the balance of her bill and walked out. The boys in the workshop were laughing so hard that tears filled their eyes.

One of the biggest orders I got at Cosmos was from a man I did not even know who walked into our shop off the street. He said, "Mr. Wiener, I want you to make me 20 sofas, all the same style." I gave him a price—$180 for each sofa. He then turned around and auctioned off the sofas, over several months, at Ames Auction House in Beverly Hills, telling everyone that each sofa came from an estate in Beverly Hills. He ripped out my label and sold the sofas for more than $500. This experience taught me that people can be very gullible. He was quite an operator and a real ace at "packaging."

When Martin Cohen put up his furniture business for sale, I bought it and changed the name to Fine Line Furniture. I now owned a 1,200 square-foot shop at 355 North Western Avenue. I printed up leaflets for the business which I passed around the neighborhood:

> Ask for Dave. Hello!!! Here I am to give you my service and our down to earth policy to satisfy you . . . This circular is our humble way of introducing ourselves, without the expenses of television and radio advertising. Here is our offer! We will give you a free estimate without any obligation on modernizing and re-upholstering your living room set, or any single piece in your home with our Down to Earth Policy: No mis-statements. No high-pressure talks or deals. Just plain honest business. Convenient time payments. Terms within your budget. . .10% off with this leaflet. Give us a call any time for a free estimate Hollywood 5—9389.

The leaflet hit on all the features that my customers wanted and before long the business was doing very well and we were able to take over the entire building. The showroom had windows facing the street and we displayed our furniture which brought customers in. Renée was working part-time and I had two decorators on the floor working for us. We sold furniture directly to interior designers, many of whom had a very high-class clientele.

One of our clients, Doris Grossman, worked in the film and television business. She came into the showroom and said, "David, I am in trouble. I am doing a big job, and nobody can do what I need and on time. We are shooting in less than two weeks."

I said, "What is the job?"

"I need draperies for Valley of the Dolls. This was a Hollywood extravaganza based on the best-selling novel by Jacqueline Susann. Doris took me to the film set and showed me the windows; they were 30 feet high.

Doris said, "We've had many decorators here and they don't want to touch the job. It's just too difficult and we need the job finished right away." I thought to myself if somebody can build the Brooklyn Bridge, if somebody can build the Empire State Building, somebody must know how to make draperies for these windows. I knew a guy who had his own business who used to work for me. His name was Manuel and he was a real expert in drapery-making. I told him, "Come with me and take a look at the job, but don't say that you work on your own. Tell them that you are my associate."

Manuel and I arrived; he looked over the job and said that he could deliver the job on time. I told Doris, "Yes, it can be done but it will be very, very expensive because it is a complicated job."

The producers said, "We don't care how much it costs. Just do it." I quoted them a price three times what it cost us to make the draperies. And I guaranteed the work. I told them if there were any mistakes we would do it over. I was never afraid that we would fail and I never said no to a job. After my experience in the camps when I said, "Yes, I am a schlosser" and I did not know the first thing about being a mechanic, I knew that I could figure a way out of almost any problem. And if not, kill me or hang me. I had no fear.

We delivered the draperies and everyone was very happy. Renée and I were invited to a party given by the producers. Neither of us was comfortable there. We "smelled garbage;" the party was not our cup of tea and we left.

That was my first foray into the entertainment business. Soon after, the Dunes Hotel in Las Vegas contacted me. The hotel's manager, Jim Hawthorne, asked me to make all the furniture for the stage shows. We used to get a ringside seat at all the shows and the hotel management sent us free whiskey and champagne. We were treated like royalty. Sometimes, three or four other couples would join us on our trips after a job had been completed. At the end of an evening when it was time to get the bill, the waiter always said, "No charge, Mr. Wiener, no charge. It's on the house." I remember that one of my friends, Jack Silver, asked me, "David, are you involved with the Mafia?" That could have been the only explanation for how well we were treated but the truth was that I just did a good job for the Dunes and the management wanted to give me special treatment for being such a reliable vendor. Renée always came with me and we used to enjoy the fancy shows with scantily clad dancers with their feather boas, and the live orchestras. Renée used to say to me, "David, if you are happy, then I am happy."

I also made furniture for some of the productions at the Los Angeles Philharmonic which was located on Fifth Street and at the legitimate theaters in Los Angeles for Broadway shows like Kiss Me Kate and The Merry Widow. The program credits used to read "Furniture Designed by David Wiener, Fine Line Furniture." I got a real kick out of seeing my name in print, but that was nothing compared to the personal joys that awaited Renée and me.

chapter eight

Put Your Hands Up

From the time that Renée and I married in 1951, we talked about having children. It was very important to me to carry on the Wiener name, and Renée felt the same way. We both wanted to have a big family. The doctors were not very optimistic that Renée could have children after everything that she had endured during the war—malnutrition and injuries—but we were both determined to try. Renée's love for me was so strong that she was willing to go against the doctor's warnings and try to have children.

Early on, Renée suffered a miscarriage; the second time that she became pregnant, we had a little baby boy, but he was very weak and only survived for eight hours. This was a crushing blow to both of us. Looking back on the years that Renée worked with me in the upholstery and furniture business, I am sure that her health had been somewhat compromised by all the hard work and long days to make a go of things.

At one point, Renée and I decided to take a break and concentrate on getting pregnant again. A new business could wait awhile. We went to Washington, D.C. and New York for a vacation. I still did not know what a "five star" hotel meant, but we stayed in very nice places, ate in good restaurants, and went to Broadway shows. It was a very good trip because Renée became pregnant in New York. Now all we had to do was hope that everything would go smoothly and that we would not be faced with yet another disappointment after so many years of trying.

In the beginning, we did not tell anyone our good news. But I drove our car very slowly and friends would ask, "Is Renée pregnant?" because I was always trying to avoid any bumps or potholes in the streets. I was so afraid that the slightest jolt might trigger another miscarriage.

Just a few months after we opened Fine Line Furniture, our first child, Helene Frances, was born on February 11, 1960. Naturally, we were overjoyed. Helene was named after my mother, Hannah, and Renée's mother, Frances. I remember the day that Renée gave birth. She was cutting expensive fabric in the shop, and her belly was literally resting on the table. All of a sudden she turned to me and said, "David, take me to the hospital." On the way she told me to stop at the delicatessen on Western Avenue and buy her a sweet roll.

Helene was born at Cedars of Lebanon Hospital. It was a joyous day for Renée and me. I used to smother Helene with kisses. Renée's Aunt Sally warned me, "David, you are going to give this child too much love." I did not care.

—what harm was there in "too much" love? No matter how tired I was when I came home from work, if Helene put her arms around my neck I just melted. She looked just like my beautiful mother and my adoring sister, Malka, with her dark hair and dark eyes. I saw the chance for a new life for our family, and a way to begin again. I now had something to live for.

Three years later, on November 17, 1963, our son, Michael, was born. I was more than happy. I was delirious—my son would carry on the Wiener name. We had a bris at our house on 6438 Drexel Avenue. Renée's uncles Aaron and Al came, and so did my brother Jacob. I served the best scotch whiskey that I could find to celebrate. Uncle Al said, "Why are you serving such good liquor?" I almost knocked his teeth out. Didn't he realize the significance of the birth of our son, Michael, whom we named after my father, Moshe? Jacob got so drunk, from happiness, that he lay down on the floor and fell asleep. Michael has red hair and he looks just like my brothers, Szyje and Yosel.

As our family flourished so did Fine Line Furniture, and now Renée and I had an even more important reason to succeed—to provide for our children so that they would not have to struggle the way we did in the early years of our lives. We would have a lot to learn about being parents and the American customs of child rearing, but one thing is for sure, there is never too much love, and we considered ourselves truly blessed from the day that each of our children were born. I suspect that being Holocaust survivors affected our parenting skills—maybe we worried too much about the children while they were growing up and expected a lot from them—but there was never a day that we did not love them or care about their well-being.

There were a lot of companies interested in becoming suppliers to Fine Line Furniture. I got a call from Paul Wood who was a salesman for Van Roger, the biggest upholstery and supply wholesaler in Los Angeles. I told Paul, "I cannot buy from Van Roger." I did not say why and he invited me to have lunch with him. I liked the guy; he was very sincere and so I agreed to meet him. I told him, point blank, "Some of your supplies are made in Germany and there is not a single Jew working in your company."

A month went by and Paul called me again, "Our credit manager wants to see you." I met him at his office downtown, and when I walked in I saw the nameplate on the credit manager's desk—Mr. Bloom who was Jewish. From that day, I agreed to do business with Van Roger, which over time became a big company listed on the New York Stock Exchange. I worked with Paul for a number of years buying supplies from him in exchange for his success in changing the hiring policies of his company. It was really a big victory.

Paul and I became very good friends, and a couple of years later I agreed to help him out of a financial bind. He was going through a divorce and he was short of cash to pay the divorce settlement. He said, "David, I am in trouble. I need a couple of thousand dollars, but if you lend me the money, I want to give you some collateral." He gave me the deed to some land that he owned up in Oroville, California, near the Russian River, 60 miles from Sacramento. This was the first piece of property that I owned, and it certainly would not be the last. The fact that I came to own it by doing a friend a favor, might have "set the stage" for a successful career in real estate some years later. It gave me my first taste of owning real estate. Paul and I also became business partners.

Fine Line Furniture, like my little family, was thriving. I kept the shop open on Thursday evenings until nine o'clock like many of the other furniture stores on Western Avenue. One evening, the telephone rang. It was Renée, "Uncle Aaron wants to see you. He just came back from Israel. I'll drive him down to the showroom and bring some dinner for you." Renée went back to the house after dropping Uncle Aaron off and bringing me a hot meal. Aaron and I sat around reminiscing. He liked me very much. I heard the doorbell ring, and a nice-looking tall fellow walked in. I asked, "Can I help you, sir?"

"No, I just want to see what you have here." We had three showrooms with bedroom sets and dining room and living room furniture. I thought that there was something fishy about him. After a few minutes of wandering around, pretending to look at the furniture, he came up to Aaron and me and said, "Please walk into your office." Then he pulled out a gun and said, "Put your hands up."

My uncle's teeth were chattering. I spoke to him in Yiddish. "Calm down, calm down. Don't do anything crazy. Take everything out of your pockets. Take off your jewelry and put it on the desk." I did the same thing. Then I told the gunman, "Sir, do me a favor. Don't hit my uncle. He is an old man. He doesn't speak English. Anything you want, I'll give to you." I opened the safe in my office. "Take whatever you want."

I knew I had to stay calm and keep my wits about me or the guy might shoot us. He took all the cash in the safe and everything that we had put on my desk; then he locked Aaron and me in the bathroom. I heard the front door close. Through the bathroom door, I heard the front door bell ring again, and another customer came into the showroom. I yelled as loudly as I could, "Help. Help." The surprised customer opened the bathroom door and let us out.

Aaron and I went back to his apartment. Renée and Aunt Sally were waiting for us there. Aaron poured himself a full glass of scotch and drank it down like it was water. A few days later, I found out that there was a hold up at Tom's Furniture Store right on Western Avenue in our neighborhood. The owners tried to fight off the intruders and one of them was hit over the head and died. When I heard this I told Renée, "I didn't come to America to be killed." I called up Barclay Auctioneers and sold off our entire inventory and closed down the company after ten successful years in business. All my friends thought I was crazy, but I believe that money does not really count—you can always make money. Money is secondary—it is life that counts.

Surviving the Holocaust, against all odds taught me the value of life and how precious each day really is. The many times I wished that I were dead just to take me out of my misery were behind me. I was no longer the 18-year old prisoner with barely a piece of bread to keep me from starving or the slave laborer with nothing more than a tin can—my only possession and the sum total of my life—from which I drank murky soup or carried water to wash my face. I was now 43 years old, a husband and father, grateful for life and the chance to breathe fresh air and embrace whatever opportunity I could discover for my precious family and myself. 1969, a new decade, was just around the corner and it was time to make a change.

chapter nine

MISTER WEE-NAH

I got out of the furniture and upholstery business and went into textiles. I opened Western Fabric Company in an 8,000 square-foot warehouse at 812 South Wall Street in downtown Los Angeles selling fabrics to the wholesale and retail trade. I did everything: I was the buyer and the salesman. I did not know any of the manufacturers but I learned very quickly by going to the Furniture Mart building. All the textile mills from around the country had representatives there and I quickly learned who was willing to sell to us, and who thought that we were just small potatoes and not worth dealing with because we did not have enough credit with the banks.

I also visited the large showrooms on the East coast, and the mills that were located mainly in the South. I wanted to find a way to buy goods at lower prices so that I could beat out the competition. I made arrangements with certain mills to buy their closeouts in order to sell textiles at competitive prices. I found a mill near Philadelphia in Wilmington, Pennsylvania where they made fabric for upholstery and men's ties. The owner, Bobby Fortinsky, helped me compete with the big boys. He was a very nice Jewish guy.

After we had concluded our business for the day I said, "Bob, I have to get to New York to visit some of the other manufacturers' representatives."

He said, "David, let's have dinner first and then I'll take you up to New York." Bob owned his own plane. No sooner than when we took off, a storm blew in, and there was loud thunder and lightning. The plane was bouncing up and down and rolling left and right. I thought that it was my last day, but we landed safely at a small airport in New Jersey. Bob had been a B-29 bomber pilot during World War II, and it was obvious that he had flown in worse conditions. But I never wanted to fly in a small plane again.

I started getting a good reputation in the textile business; some of the mills were extending me credit and before long we outgrew our warehouse on South Wall Street and moved to a 20,000 square-foot space on 1234 South Maple Avenue in downtown Los Angeles. I hired five salesmen to cover six western states: Idaho, California, Washington, Oregon, Iowa, and Nevada. The business was doing well but all the profits were going back into inventory. I took Paul Wood in as a partner; he coordinated sales for our entire territory and was a very successful salesman.

Running a textile business—or any business—is not just about buying inventory and filling orders. You have to have a good relationship with the people that work for you from the salespeople to the stock boys. Sometimes, you get involved in their personal lives. That has certainly been true for me.

Three of the guys working in the warehouse were Latino—Juan, Luis, and Victor—and they always showed up to work on time, and did a good job. I did not suspect that anything was wrong with any of them until Victor's wife called me up on the telephone sobbing, "Mr. Wiener, you haven't paid my husband his wages for this week."

I called Victor into my office. "Victor, what did you do with your salary?"

"Mr. Wiener, I went out drinking with the boys." He told me that it was his routine to go to a bar with his buddies a few blocks from our warehouse after he got paid on Fridays.

Every Friday night, my family had Shabbat dinner together. I called Renée and told her, "Tonight I am not coming home for dinner. You and the kids, go ahead and eat without me. I am going to a bar with the boys." I went to the bar with the Luis, Victor, and Juan and matched them drink for drink. Eventually, Victor was sprawled out on the floor.

The following Monday morning I called Victor into my office. I asked him, "Is it worth losing everything for booze? Don't screw up your life.

You're a good kid and you can have a future in this business. I'll make you a salesman." I sent him to Boyle Heights to cover the stores which, by this time, were mainly owned by Latinos. He was a very good salesman and I trusted him.

Victor told me that his parents wanted to see who this Mr. Wiener is. We flew to Mexico, and Renée went with us. His parents threw a big party with a mariachi band and served us a real feast—a whole pig roasted in a pit in the ground. His parents thanked me for saving their son from alcohol. I gave Victor my trust and an opportunity for a better life and he never let me down.

Eventually, Victor used to go into Tijuana to sell fabric for me and he established a loyal clientele there. I'd sometimes go with Victor to Tijuana to collect our money and generate sales. I was really proud of him and he knew that; he used to call me his father and tell our customers, "Mr. Wiener is better to me than my own father." It is always amazing what a difference one person can make in someone else's life just by giving them good advice and setting them straight.

I remember that another employee asked me to lend him $200 to buy a car. No sooner had I given him the money, then he disappeared. I figured that was the last I would see of him or my money. But two years later, he called me from Texas, and said, "Mr. Wiener, you are the best friend I ever had." A few days later a check arrived in the mail. He paid me back.

And it wasn't only Latino kids that I took under my wing. One day the telephone rang at my office. It was one of my survivor acquaintances and we were pretty good friends. "David, meet me at Cantor's Deli for lunch. I need a favor from you."

"David, put my son, Simon, to work. He's lazy. He doesn't want to stay in college and I can't figure out what's wrong with him." I told him to send his son down to Western Fabric and I would give him a job. I also taught him an important lesson in life.

The warehouse was jumping. We were selling fabrics to wholesale furniture manufacturers and directly to retail stores. Woolworth's was now one of our big customers. I told my foreman, Luis, "Don't let Simon sit on a chair for one minute. Give him the hardest work. Let him schlep heavy bolts of cloth, sweep the floor—whatever needs doing. Just keep the kid working." After about two weeks, Simon came into my office. He said, "Mr. Wiener, I can't take it anymore."

I told him, "Listen, I'll give you an easy job if you promise to buckle down and study hard. I'll even help you out." He went back to college and became a lawyer. He realized that it was a lot easier to use your brains than to do backbreaking work, day in and day out, and here is the best part of the story:

Years later, my son, Michael graduated from Loyola Law School and he was interviewing for his first job. He got an interview at Manatt, Phelps and Phillips, one of the most prominent law firms in Los Angeles. One of the associates started asking him routine questions.

"Where did you go to law school?" And what is your name? And then the guy threw him a curve ball. "Was your father in the textile business in downtown Los Angeles?" Michael answered yes. Then the interviewer said, "I used to work for your father and he helped me out. My name is Simon." Michael was offered a job with the firm in the creditors' rights department.

At Rosh Hashanah, Michael and I were sitting together in synagogue. He tapped me on the shoulder and whispered, "Do you know a guy named Simon? He says that he used to work for you."

I looked down at my tallit and thought for a moment. I have a pretty good memory for names and I said, "Simon, Simon, yeah, I remember him. I nearly kicked him out of the warehouse because he was such a complainer, but he shaped up." Michael told me, "Well, he's my boss now."

In less than five years, Western Fabric became the largest textile distributor west of the Mississippi. We carried all kinds of novelty fabrics. My partner, Paul Wood, said, "Our customers are asking for fake fur. How do we get it cheaply?"

I told him, "Wait a minute. Don't worry. You want fake fur. I'll get you fake fur." I spent a few days in New York City where I had made some good connections with Malden Mills in Massachusetts, Borg Fur from Wisconsin, and Furtex in New York and I was able to buy fake fur from the suppliers at less than wholesale. We could pass on the savings to our customers and beat out the competition. For a while fake fur was the hottest item in the textile industry. There were fake fur pillows, coats, bedspreads, and toys in all colors of the rainbow. I became known as Los Angeles' King of Fake Fur. Eventually, its popularity wore off, and we had to find the next "hot" item.

I felt very comfortable doing business in New York City. The South was a different kettle of fish. One of the biggest mills was the Milliken Textile Company; the owners were reputed to be members of the John Birch Society. I did not want to do business with the company.

Other mills had their regular customers that they were used to selling to, but I found a way to break in and get good prices through negotiating southern style. You had to get close to the general managers and you had to have an intermediary with a real Southern pedigree. Otherwise, you were just a foreigner in their eyes.

I used to fly from New York to Greensboro, North Carolina and meet up with a textile broker, Teddy Summit, who knew every hole in the wall joint, and every mill where we could make a good deal. Teddy was a good 'ole Southern Jewish boy—third generation. I could spend six or seven hours in the car with him driving from mill to mill and he never repeated the same joke twice. He had the strangest habit of wearing socks that did not match. I think that that was his trademark. He also gave me some good tips on how to negotiate with the general managers and what to watch out for.

I visited a mill in Greensboro, North Carolina that I really wanted to do business with. When I walked into the general manager's office, he was not particularly welcoming. After a few minutes of stilted conversation, he said, "Mister WEE-NAH. You want to do business with us. See this drawer. I am going to go to the bathroom. When I come back, if I like what I see in the drawer, we'll do business together." Teddy Summit had tipped me off about this practice, and I put an envelope with cash in it in the desk drawer. The general manager came back, counted the money, and said, "O.K., Yankee, I guess that you and I can do some business together." He opened a bottle of good Southern bourbon and we made a toast.

Southerners believed that every Yankee was a real sucker. It was a regional bias—maybe they thought that the Civil War had not really settled things between the North and the South. I always had to be on the lookout for someone who might be trying to take advantage of me—let's say just misrepresenting the cost or the amount of goods that they were selling me.

I'd say, "How many yards are in this warehouse?" And the owner would tell me that it was 60,000 yards of material. I'd measure the material by pacing the floor and figure out the total square footage, and usually, they tried to short me, sometimes by as much as 30,000 yards, if I wasn't careful. I never allowed a mill manager to ship the material to me. I had two trucks. I'd watch them load the trucks and lock them up right away and have my drivers head straight for Los Angeles while I was still at the mill. I used to take the keys to the back of the trucks because I paid for everything in cash and I wanted to be sure that no one would steal the merchandise along the way.

I also did business with two Jewish brothers from Georgia who owned a big distribution warehouse packed with textiles from different mills throughout the region. The Lewises were the biggest suppliers of textile to Sears & Roebuck. Both brothers had hearts of gold. Their father was a Russian refugee; he came to the United States after World War I and the whole family was very successful. They used to extend me unlimited credit if I couldn't pay for the merchandise immediately which was a big help in growing my business. Bernie, one of the brothers, was a gambler and flew his own plane to Las Vegas. He used to wear beautiful, blue suits and dressed like a real playboy. When he came to Los Angeles, he sometimes stayed with Renée and me.

I usually flew back from North Carolina through New York on my way back to Los Angeles to see mill representatives from other parts of the country. Sometimes I'd even make a roundtrip in one day. Renée used to tell me that I was working too hard, but I liked the game for a while, at least.

I learned that it was "all a game" from David Friedman, who had a showroom on Broadway and 32nd Street, right in the heart of the textile and garment districts of Manhattan. The guy was a multi-multi-millionaire; he and his brothers had made a fortune selling material for uniforms to the U.S. military during World War II. He was a real tough negotiator and he loved every minute of it. When I met him in his office, I asked him, "Dave, just give me three cents off your price per yard, and that will pay for my trip to New York."

He was jumping up and down, "No way, David. I don't care if you are starving. That's it." His wife was watching all of this, and I think that she really liked me and wanted her husband to give me a break in the price but she did not have any say in the matter. I left his office and went back to my hotel. I was really angry.

At seven thirty that evening, the phone rang in my hotel room. I answered it. "Mr. Wiener, this is Mr. Friedman's chauffeur. He'd like you to join him for dinner." I told him to come back in half an hour although I really had a mind just to blow the whole thing off. I guess that I did not want to walk away and waste a trip so I went. The chauffeur picked me up and drove me to a very fancy restaurant in Times Square. David Friedman was sitting at a table with a bottle of champagne on ice. "David, order anything you want." I felt very uncomfortable; I felt like a real schlepper sitting next to him.

When we finished dinner, David turned to me, "You're missing the point. In negotiations, I win, not you." After that I did business with him. He was a Yankee son-of-a-bitch. He had a very small mind. The deal was more important to him than the money, but I learned how to negotiate with him, and he eventually gave me a pretty good price. But sometimes, his attitude made my blood boil. Renée used to say to me, "David, calm down. You're going to have a heart attack one of these days if you let people like David Friedman get to you."

Western Fabric moved into a 60,000 square-foot warehouse on Second Street, and I had a large crew of young boys working for me. People knew that the business was doing pretty well. I received a call from a friend, Mary Freeman, who had been in the camps with me during the Holocaust. She said, "David, my husband, Marvin, is temporarily out of work. Could you hire him for a short time?" I knew what it was like to need a helping hand and I said, "Tell your husband to come down to the warehouse. I can put him to work." I was about to leave for another buying trip to New York.

I called Marvin into my office. "Marvin, do me a favor. I want you to watch the front door and the back door. Nothing else. If anyone comes in for a pick-up or a delivery, make sure that they sign for it. I want to be sure that we keep track of who is going in and out and that nothing gets stolen."

Marvin looked at me. "David, I never did that before. I am afraid that I might make a mistake."

I told him, "Marvin, I trust you. There is nothing to it. Listen to me carefully. Whatever you do, one thing is for sure, if you make a mistake no one will hang you, and no one will shoot you." Years later, whenever I see Marvin's son, Joe, who is a lawyer, he likes to remind me of what I said to his father. The point of this story is that some people fear doing something new. They don't believe in my motto, "If he can do it, I can do it." Experience is the best teacher and builds confidence—even selling bananas and tomatoes at a swap meet. Experience also teaches you when it is time to make a change and look for a new business challenge.

chapter ten

DAFKA

I owned Western Fabric for ten years. Over time, it became harder and harder to make a decent profit. The big guys were trying to squeeze out the middle-size guys like me and in order to maintain market share I had to hire more salespeople to hold on to my territories. It was becoming a real headache and my partner, Paul Wood, and I really had had enough. We knew when it was time to get out. We closed Western Fabric in 1979.

It is strange how opportunities sometimes present themselves that totally change the course of your life. You just have to be able to recognize them and see them for what they are—a new beginning with a great upside.

While I was still operating Western Fabric, I received a call from Jim Lloyd, a real estate broker at Coldwell Banker. He said, "Mr. Wiener, you own a piece of land in Fontana. Is it for sale?" Some years earlier, I started buying vacant land as an investment.

I said, "Yes. Come and see me."

Fontana is about 60 miles east of Los Angeles and was the headquarters for the only Kaiser Steel mill west of the Mississippi. The mill was in continuous operation until the 1980s when foreign competition forced its closure. There were also a lot of chicken farms and orange groves in the area. With the construction of the San Bernardino Freeway, the entire region was slowly evolving from a farm and industrial community, to a community of renters and homeowners who were employed in Fontana and other cities in San Bernardino and Riverside Counties. I figured that if someone was interested in our property, something big was about to happen in the area.

I owned a 25% interest in the property. Al Freilich, Renée's uncle, owned 50%, and Henry Teichman, who was a Holocaust survivor, owned the remaining 25%. We paid $99,000 for the land and took out a loan with payments of $167 each a month plus the property.

I met Jim at a Chinese restaurant on 2nd Street in downtown Los Angeles next to my warehouse. "I have a client who wants to offer you six hundred and fifty thousand dollars for the property."

I told Jim, "Let me think about. I don't know if we are ready to sell."

My kids wanted me to sell the property but, Henry said, "Let's wait and see what's going to happen in the area." Uncle Al was ready to sell his share to me. I agreed to pay him $500,000 for his 50% interest, so now I owned a 75% interest in the property.

Then, I got another call from Jim Lloyd. "I'd like to talk with you." I sat down with him and he said that his client authorized him to offer us $750,000 for the land.

I asked him, "Jim, do me a favor. Be my friend. Who is the buyer?" "Savon Pharmacy wants to buy the property." I had never heard of Savon. I drove around Los Angeles and saw a number of their stores and I liked what I saw. They were a big national chain, so they must have evaluated the area and decided that Fontana had potential. The property was becoming "hot" and soon after I got a call from one of the biggest developers in Santa Monica. He said, "Mr. Wiener, we'd like to offer you $1,200,000 for your Fontana property."

I said, "Let me think about it." It was certainly a lot of money and most people would probably have taken the deal. But I had other plans. I wanted to develop the land myself. I did not know anything about real estate development, but I knew that my future was in real estate. I wanted to get out of the textile business altogether. I offered to buy Henry out. He was reluctant to sell his share in the land but he did not want to be my partner any longer. I offered him $375,000 for his 25 percent interest which was above market value. Now I owned the land free and clear.

I went to see the president of Manufacturers Bank, Sam Simon, who had been my banker for many years while I was in the textile business. I asked Sam, "Do me a favor. Help me out. I want to build a shopping center on the land I own in Fontana."

He looked at me, "David, are you crazy? You don't know the first think about the construction business." He just about kicked me out of his office. I went to another banker and he said, "You should take in a partner who has a track record in real estate development. That will give you credibility." I knew a guy named Jim Chappell, who was also a banker, but I did not know where he was. I wrote him a letter at an old address that I had for him and said, "Jim, where are you? I need you now. Please call." I waited. A week later, Jim called me up because the letter had been forwarded to his new address. We arranged to meet for lunch. I told him of my intentions to build a shopping center and that I needed about $900,000 to pay off the existing mortgage and to cover construction costs.

"But David you have no tenants and no experience in the shopping center business."

I told him, "Savon Pharmacy is interested. Let's meet with Jim Lloyd at Coldwell Banker. He can verify their interest and there are other companies who want space on my land. I think that we can come up with a plan that will support a loan. If it's legit, fine, and if not we can just forget the whole thing."

I arranged a luncheon meeting with Jim Lloyd and Jim Chappell. Jim Lloyd said, "I can get you a letter of intent that Savon will go in there and Lucky's Stores as well. They'll be your two anchors." Jim Chappell said, "Give me a few days, and I'll see what the bank is willing to do for you, David."

A few days later, the doorbell rang at my home in Beverly Hills. It was Jim Chappell holding a bottle of champagne. "Well, David, we have a deal." I was speechless.

Now that I had the money I had to find a builder to help me develop the land. I envisioned a 122,000 square foot shopping center on Sierra Avenue and Marygold Avenue, a major intersection in Fontana. I was introduced to Herb Lundin from Thousand Oaks. He had a good track record as a builder of shopping centers. I hired him to advise me and help develop the property. I put him in charge of construction and I went out and signed up all the tenants. In the middle of construction Herb left the project and I had to finish construction on my own. While the shopping center was under construction, I used to sleep in one of the stores that had been completed so that I would be there when the construction crew arrived at six o'clock in the morning.

Renée used to come out and pick me up at the end of the week, when we would take a little break by driving to Palm Springs. Neither of us could believe that Fontana Plaza belonged to us but the "will to work" paid off. I was able to complete the shopping center and sign up some very good tenants: Miller's Outpost, Fayva Shoes, Goodman's Jewelers, Shakey's Pizza, Crafty Lady, California Pants, and a Hallmark card shop in addition to Lucky's and Savon. I survived and began to thrive.

Getting tenants wasn't always easy. I wanted to bring a Sizzler's Restaurant into the shopping center. Every week I went to visit the regional manager, Bill Williams. Without fail, he would throw me out of his office. Finally, persistence paid off and I got the chance to see him. "Mr. Williams, move into a space in my center. In two years, if you don't succeed there, I'll give you back all the money that you paid on improvements and tear up the lease."

He looked at me and said, "You are a spicy son-of-a-bitch." It was really a deal that he couldn't turn down and it became one of the most successful Sizzler's Restaurants in the chain.

I was in an expansionist frame of mind. I looked at some property near Fontana Plaza at the corner of Foothill and Sierra Boulevards that was in foreclosure. Downey Savings Bank was holding the property. The only two tenants on the property were Thrifty's Drug Store and Pizza Hut, leaving about 69,000 square feet of vacant space. I bought the property, negotiated a lease with Kragen Auto Supply and Lucky's Market, adding another 23,000 square feet of rented space. In a few months the entire space was fully leased at Foothill and Sierra Plaza.

Then I learned that there were about four acres of vacant land across the street from Fontana Plaza. I made a deal with the president of National

Lumber, Mr. Jaffe, to put up a 70,000 square-foot building for the company, but I didn't own all the land necessary to accommodate the size of the building. After Mr. Jaffee signed a lease with me, he said, "David, are you crazy, you signed a lease with me and you don't have control of all the land that we need."

I told him, "Don't worry, Mr. Jaffee. I'll get it." I flew to Virginia to see the landowner and bought the adjacent three acres to satisfy the terms of the deal. The owner was the "best poker player" I ever met, and I was really sweating bullets while I was in negotiation with him. My lawyer, my banker, and my accountant advised me not to build there. They said that I would be taking a big risk. I told them in Yiddish, "Dafka—in spite of you, I am going to build." I had no fear. I felt that I really had nothing to lose and I believed that "if one person can make a go of something, so can I." That has always been my philosophy.

Failure means nothing to me. Possessions mean nothing; money means nothing. Making money—the challenge of a deal—that is what interests me. I also always believed that I did not want to let the family down. As a child in Lodz my parents always said, "Worship God and keep the family together." These were the two most important principles of their life. At least I can say that I worked hard to keep the family together. The part about God has been a more difficult commandment to uphold.

After a number of years, National Lumber went out of business. I had the vision to convert the space into an indoor swap meet—a business that I really knew something about from my days in Lodi, New Jersey selling soap, bananas, and tomatoes. Once the conversion was made, I offered the space to my daughter and her husband, Jon. He took over the space and has been running an indoor swap meet business to this day. He works six days a week and he is doing a very good job.

My reputation as a developer in the city was growing and people started calling me the King of Fontana—I had traded in fake fur for real estate and earned a new name. Contemplating the history of the Jews in the United States, it was not that unusual for people to progress from street peddler to owners of garment and textile businesses to real estate. As a people who were prohibited from owning land in Eastern Europe, going into real estate was one of the many freedoms that this country has afforded Jews. And later the professions (banker, lawyer, accountant) opened their doors slowly to the next generation. My son, Michael, fulfilled my boyhood aspirations of someday becoming a lawyer.

I kept on expanding my holdings in Fontana throughout the 1980s. Just before the prime interest rate reached 21 percent and the real estate market hit a bump, I developed a 72,000 square-foot project that I named County Square. The County of San Bernardino leased 40,000 square feet for government employees, and I tried to lease up the rest of the space to small proprietors, but I could only lease about 35% of the remaining property.

I got behind on my payments to a large Texas insurance company that held the mortgage on some of my properties which served as the collateral on the loan. Predictably, I received a letter from the lender threatening foreclosure.

I called the regional manager of the insurance company, Mr. Wood, numerous times and he would not take my calls so I wrote him many letters. He finally picked up the telephone and said, "Mr. Wiener, you signed a note for twenty-two million five hundred thousand dollars. You are responsible for paying it back," and then he hung up. Then I wrote Mr. Wood one last letter:

Listen, Mr. Wood. I want to talk to you. You keep hanging up on me. Let me first mention a couple of things. The war is over. Japan and America made peace after World War II. Israel and Germany made peace. Russia and America made peace. We can make peace, too.

That got a response. "Mr. Wiener, you know how to write a good letter. I am going to come out and see you." He was a big, brawny Texan with a thick accent. Over lunch, he told me, "Look Mr. Wiener, if I renegotiate the terms of our loan with you, I am going to have to do the same thing for everyone who is having a hard time. And frankly, I see no reason to make an exception in your case. We have a big loan portfolio, and a lot of borrowers are having a difficult time right now." And then he left.

I consulted with a number of top lawyers in Los Angeles and most of them advised me to file for Chapter eleven. One lawyer offered to take on my case but I did not believe that he had the stomach to win. I told my son, Michael, "I am going to negotiate on my own behalf."

I flew to Texas without an appointment. I told the secretary, "I am not moving until I see Mr. Wood." She picked up the phone and told him that I was in the outer office. After a few minutes, she said to me, "Can you come back tomorrow? I'll give you a call at your hotel and tell you when he can see you." (This story is beginning to sound familiar.) I was staying at the Hyatt Hotel not far from his office. I went to the hotel bar and had a few drinks and thought about what I was going to offer him in exchange for a workout on the loan.

I went up to my hotel room and called Michael and then Renée. She told me, "Don't worry, David. We'll make it. I know that you will figure something out." She had so much faith in me. She was truly the best partner that any man could have had. Our relationship was one that went way beyond love—I am not a literary person so sometimes my choice of words may not be very poetic—between us we had a bond that was stronger than any chain.

Mr. Wood's secretary called me later that evening and told me to be at his office at ten o'clock the next morning. He had an office that was more than 30 feet long. There were seven people sitting around a conference table when I walked in carrying a plain suitcase with all my documents inside. I felt like a fly drowning in a big bowl of soup.

Mr. Wood started the meeting. One of the lawyers asked me, "Mr. Wiener, where is your lawyer?"

"Do I need a lawyer? Are you going to hurt me?" I think that they were mildly amused.

I took a deep breath and made my offer, "I want you to discount my mortgage to sixteen million dollars. The underlying property is worth more than sixty million dollars, and your mortgage is twenty-two million five hundred thousand. I will give you a half million dollars right now in exchange for a ninety-day extension on the mortgage which will give me time to refinance the mortgage at a better interest rate. I will try to raise the money in that time. If I can't, I will give you another two hundred thousand dollars for an additional sixty-day extension. If at the end of that period

I can't find another lender, the properties are yours. I will just walk away and you will own the three Fontana shopping centers."

The room was completely silent except for the sound of shuffling papers. I could not tell what Mr. Wood's reaction was. He would have made a pretty good poker player, but this was not a game of cards and I stood to lose a lot if the deal I had put on the table was not accepted—it was a real gamble.

I went back to the hotel and within a few hours, I got a call from Mr. Wood. "We have a deal, Mr. Wiener. Come back tomorrow. The lawyers will draw up the papers."

I was able to get a new loan from an East Coast lender for $18 million on better terms and I paid off the insurance company that agreed to discount their loan by $5 million in exchange for the accelerated payments. The entire Los Angeles real estate industry was talking about this deal. Everyone in the real estate business thought it was impossible to do anything like this. But somehow, necessity always brings out the best in me, and I was able to come up with a creative solution to a big problem. I eventually rented up all the empty stores and all the space in the shopping centers is full and there is ample cash flow to carry the debt.

I saw that there was a real demand for rental apartments in Fontana. I built 375 apartment units on Marigold, Juniper, and Foothill Boulevards. I did everything from A to Z without the help of any outside partners—I acquired the land, acted as the general contractor, and leased the apartments working from six o'clock in the morning until eight o'clock at night. With all the real estate that I owned in Fontana, I had to open an office there and I hired two women to work for me to take care of collecting the rents and doing the bookkeeping. One of the women, Betty Lou Strauss, worked for me for over 20 years driving all the way from the San Fernando Valley.

About three years ago, my son, Michael came into my office. He asked me, "Dad, do you need my help?"

I said, "What took you so long?" Now Michael is running DW Development from our offices in Beverly Hills on Beverly Drive and we are temporarily out of the development business. We mainly manage the properties that we still have in our real estate portfolio. If any of our tenants has a complaint, Michael takes care of it. I just go into the office to give everybody a headache. I miss the excitement of the business, but my body is starting to get old. I am like my customer, Mrs. McCue, who told me many years ago, "My heart wants to dance, but my legs won't let me."

chapter eleven

PROCLAIMING ISRAEL'S NAME

Some days I feel that my life is very empty, that I have no purpose. When I was working 12 to 14 hours a day I always had a goal. From my mother and father, I was always taught to be productive—to do something useful with my life. And I always had the stamina to take on any business challenge. I don't feel that way today—I am slowing down, but I have found other pursuits that give me satisfaction, and that has been to give back to charitable organizations, to find ways to contribute to the betterment of relations between Jews and gentiles and to help Israel. Apart from my family, these are the most important commitments that I have made in my life in the past few years since I have given up the day-to-day challenges of the real estate business—chasing after the next "impossible deal" that I made happen through sheer guts and persistence.

I have always loved music so it was very natural that I became a benefactor of Young Artists International, an organization that brings young, gifted gentile musicians from Eastern Europe to perform in Israel with young Israeli musicians. In March 2006, I went to Israel with my present wife, Lila Gilbert, along with four other couples from the United States to concerts in Eilat and Jerusalem. The soloist was Ida Haendel who studied with violinist Yasha Haifitz. As I listened to the music, my mind went back to a happy time when I played the violin with my brother, Jacob, a time when I had the luxury to dream about a future full of possibilities that every child deserves. I thought about all the Jewish children who had been killed in the Holocaust who could have been composers, musicians, and doctors—you name it. They are not here, but I felt good that the concert hall was filled and the audience cheered when they heard the music.

The concert in Eilat was dedicated to the memory of 39-year old Jewish journalist Daniel Pearl, who was assassinated by Muslim extremists in Karachi, Pakistan in 2002. He was a music lover, and a devout Jew. His last words before he was murdered were, "I am a Jew."

After the concert, all the sponsors had lunch with the mayor of Eilat, Yitzchak Halevi, and the Egyptian Consul General, Ashraf el Sherbenni. He asked me to come with him to Cairo. I told him, "I am not that gutsy—a Jew in Egypt, forget it." He assured me that if I traveled with him nothing would happen but I wasn't feeling very courageous knowing about the virulent anti-Semitism in Egypt.

In Jerusalem, the gentile musicians all took a tour of Yad Vashem, the memorial to the six million Jews who died in the Holocaust. My father's name is among those recorded there.

Located on Har HaZikaron, the Mount of Remembrance, Yad Vashem is a vast complex of buildings—one of which has an eternal burning flame; another is a hall of mirrors with a tape recording of the names of the children who perished. And written on one of the walls in Hebrew is "And to them will I give in my house and within my walls a memorial and a name (Yad Vashem) that shall not be cut off." Seeing Yad Vashem is a must for anyone who visits Israel, and it was especially important that these gifted musicians be among its visitors so that they could bring back the stories of their experience to their countries where many of their people did not really have a good understanding of the history of the Holocaust or what happened during the war. As music touches the soul, so too does Yad Vashem.

After the trip, some of the musicians wrote letters of appreciation. One in particular stands out:

> *Just two days I came home . . .next day after my arrival to Mannheim from Israel, I went to Frankfurt for the festival, where I played Kodaly duo and Schubert's C Major Quintet. Now I came to Gdansk, where I am able to find peace for practicing. . . in one*

week I am playing Bach G Minor. I miss Israel. People I spent time with, our work, our concerts. Contact with the maestro gives me strength for the next months and assures me that I took right path in my life. Thank you.

Robert Kowalski
Violinist/Poland

When Lila and I were in Jerusalem, we went out to dinner and I ordered a large bottle of vodka for the table. Everyone was singing Russian and Hebrew songs. I was probably singing the loudest. Before too long all the diners in the restaurant joined in. It was very emotional for me and it brought back memories of past trips to Israel with Renée and the children.

In 2002, I lost my dear wife Renée suddenly in a tragic accident. I still cannot speak about her death. I also lost my only remaining brother, Jacob about 30 years ago when he was just 63. He died suddenly and unexpectedly of a heart attack. As I have said before, Jacob had a very tough life; he never really recovered from what the war did to him. Losing his wife, Irene took an enormous toll on his spirit and created a big hole in his heart. Jacob did remarry but it was a marriage of comfort, not love, and after a short time, he and his wife divorced. No one could replace Irene. Jacob never really reached his potential, but I know that he was proud of me, which was of some consolation. In his eyes, I succeeded on behalf of our lost brothers and sisters. Renée and Jacob are buried next to one another in the Mt. Sinai Mortuary in North Hollywood.

One of the many indelible lessons that I learned during the war is that you can lose someone in an instant—a friend lies down on the floor to go to sleep and the next morning, he is frozen to death. Life and death are but a few degrees from one another. The deep sadness for unimagined and immeasurable losses—both past and present—cast an invisible shadow over the happiness I felt sitting among the revelers in Jerusalem, and it is a shadow that will follow me, sometimes vividly, sometimes faintly for the remaining days of my life.

I have tried to do everything that I can to promote Israel's reputation among young people. A few years ago, I sponsored an Anti-Defamation

League trip of American college educators to Eastern Europe and Israel so that the students would learn that the Holocaust really happened, and that they should not accept "Holocaust deniers" as advertisers and writers in their newspapers. These young people are the future and what they believe will affect how academics, and even American policy makers view Israel. I hope that this has made some difference. It is important that people talk about what happened. For too long people remained silent. But now with "Schindler's List" and the efforts of Steven Spielberg and others like Elie Wiesel, survivors are coming forward to tell their stories. For so long, we were just afraid that people would not believe us and there were those inquisitors who made us feel guilty that we had survived when so many others had been murdered. Their questions were often tinged with suspicion about what we might have done.

I survived the war so that I could see my parents again and tell my story someday—to let people know the cruelty and inhumane treatment that I had endured along with so many others at the bloodied hands of the Nazis and their collaborators. That is what ultimately kept me going—to tell the world what I had seen. But it has taken me almost 60 years to do so willingly. There is more that I could say, but people would not believe what I went through—the pain and suffering and human degradation. And in spite of it all, I became a decent human being with compassion for others, thanks to my loving and supportive family.

I have donated ambulances to Israel especially now that the war between Israel and her neighbors has reached the boiling point. I donated one of the ambulances in Renée's memory.

Peace in the Middle East seems more elusive than ever but peace must come someday. I believe that six million Jewish lives paid for the state of Israel, and as American Jews we must do everything that we can to insure its safety and stability. Israel gives the Jewish people honor and respect. We are no longer second-class people without a real homeland. There is someone to speak for us and that is Israel—we are no longer the peddler, the wandering Jew. Israel has a strong army and a strong navy. We can be proud that we can fight and take care of ourselves and we have the backing of the United States President, George W. Bush. He is a real friend to Israel, because he knows that Israel can be counted on to fight against the extremist enemies of the Middle East and the anti-Semites around the world who want to push Israel into the sea, and destroy the United States.

Some years ago, I went to Israel for Yom Kippur. I wanted to go to a synagogue but there were no seats. I mentioned my father's name to the ushers, and they quickly found a place for me. As I sat listening to the most sacred of Jewish prayers, I thought, "Moshe Chaim, your son is alive." I am reminded of an inscription on a memorial in the Jewish cemetery in Budapest, "Hate killed them, but love keeps their memory alive." And so too do I keep the memory of my father alive in my heart.

I also went to Israel in 1973 for the commemoration of Israel's 25th anniversary. I told Renée of my plans to go alone and she understood why I felt the need to make the trip. It would have been difficult for us to take the children since Helene and Michael were both in school at the time.

I arrived at the Hilton Hotel in Tel Aviv. The city was jammed with Jews from all over the world who had come to take part in the celebration. No sooner had I checked into my room at the Hilton Hotel than I got a call from the front desk. "Mr. Wiener, we are completely sold out. There is a gentleman at the desk from South America. Would you be willing to share your room with him?" I said, "Sure, bring him up. Don't worry."

An hour later the phone rang again with the same request. By the end of the evening there were six guys sleeping on my hotel room floor. At six o'clock the next morning they all disappeared. There was a big military parade with people from all over the world standing behind barricades—I even saw Japanese people. That night there was dancing in the streets with klezmer music playing on every street corner. I was dancing like there was no tomorrow.

After three days, I traveled to Jerusalem and visited the Wailing Wall. A guy with a beard came over to me and asked me for money to help out the children. I gave him some money. About a half hour later another guy came over to me and asked me for money and I did not refuse him either. A few minutes later someone pointed to a sign posted near the wall, "Don't you see what it says? You are not supposed to give money to anyone at the wall." I told him not to bother me, I did not care, I was going to do it anyway.

I spoke to him in English. "What were you doing in the war?" He said, "I was in the camps."

"I was in the camps, too. Which camp?" "I was in Auschwitz and Deblin."

He looked me right in the eyes. He said, "Is your name Dufce?" I answered yes.

"Were you the cook in the Deblin camp? I couldn't believe my ears. He went on, "When you escaped from the train, we all heard shots. We thought that you were dead. I can't believe that you are alive and we are here together." It was a miracle that we had found one another after so many years. He was living in Minnesota and he was in Israel with his wife for the celebration.

He asked me, "What are you doing tonight?" I told him that I had no plans.

"Well, why don't you join my wife and me? We are going to a night club."

That evening, when I walked into the club, I heard somebody yelling from across the room, "David Wiener, David Wiener." I looked around and saw a guy that I knew in the furniture business from Los Angeles. He had come to Israel for the celebration, too.

I found my host and his wife and we spent the evening dancing, singing and drinking. It felt like the world belonged to us. He gave me his card with his address in Minnesota. Unfortunately, I lost it and I cannot remember his name.

chapter twelve

A New Branch of the Family Tree

Renée and I always wanted to have a big family, but malnutrition and other injuries that she suffered during the war, made it difficult for her to have children. When Helene was born on February 11, 1960 and Michael on November 17, 1963, we considered their births a real miracle. I have spoken of this before but it bears repeating.

By the time Michael was born, Renée worked part time with me, and found a babysitter to take care of the children until she came home from work. When I opened Western Fabric she stayed home full time to take care of the children, although she always acted as my confidante and greatest supporter. I saw Michael and Helene as a new branch of the Wiener family tree. I remember that I used to come home from work so tired, just dragging my feet, but seeing my children gave me an immediate lift. I'd sometimes talk to myself, "See, you could not destroy us. Life will go on."

Both Renée and I were devoted parents to Helene and Michael—you might say that we sometimes spoiled them. We did the best that we could. When I came to this country I had no education and not a penny in my pocket. When the war broke out I was really a child myself—just 13 years old—and I really had no one to guide me in how to be a father. For six years, I lived with people who often resorted to behaviors driven by the instinct to survive. I saw the worst of human cruelty perpetuated by the Nazis. From day to day, I did not know what was going to happen. The only foundation I had for living is what I learned from my mother and father when I was a young child. My father was very strict with all of his children and taught us to respect and honor our parents. In Yiddish the word that he used to say to us is D'Heretz (respect and honor). As poor as we were, my father demanded respect—he did not have a penny in his pocket, but he was always proud of himself for the way that he conducted his life. These memories stayed with me throughout the war and have been the guiding principles of my life, which I have tried to instill in my children. Honor thy father and thy mother and do good deeds for others.

Renée did not have any models for parenting either. Her parents left her in a hospital in Belgium when the war broke out. Her mother went back to Poland and probably died there; and one of her sisters and her husband perished in Auschwitz. Her other sister is mentally retarded and lives on a farm in Belgium. Renée really had no experience of what it was like to have loving parents who took care of her, but in her life, she had an abundance of love to give to her children and grandchildren. She was the best wife that any man could hope for.

Renée and I rarely shared with our children the details of what happened to us during the war while they were growing up. We did not want them to be burdened by our history. But I am sure that despite our silence, some of what we went through came across to them. There is an expression that says, "Who you are speaks so loudly that I cannot hear what you are saying." Every now and then I did mention something to the children what happened to me, and when I did tell them of some incident, I would go into our bedroom, look in the mirror and ask myself, "How can you lie to your own kids?" I didn't believe that I could have endured what happened to me and still be a half-normal person with compassion for others.

Our daughter, Helene, went to Jewish Day School on Third Street and then went to a public school while attending Hebrew school. She wanted to learn Yiddish formally, so she enrolled in classes at the University of Judaism. Up until the time that she was 13, she was very feminine, but then she really began to act more like a tomboy in my eyes—she loved baseball, and volleyball, and had a real competitive spirit. I insisted that Helene receive her bat mitzvah at a conservative synagogue, Mogen David on Pico Boulevard. Afterwards, she really did not involve herself in Judaism. It really did not hold much meaning for her.

Helene was a talented pianist. Sometimes, when I came home from work she would sit down at the piano and play some Chopin for me. I felt like I was in heaven listening to her. Her piano teacher and I believed that she could have been a concert pianist but she resented practicing and gave up the piano for sports. Renée and Helene had the usual "mother-daughter" friction. I remember tiffs about cleaning up her room, typical teenage things, but Helene was basically a good girl. She enrolled at Cal State Northridge, commuting from home. She studied accounting; obviously, she had inherited my ability in mathematics, but she wanted to become an independent woman, and she left the house. I really was crushed but she wanted to live with a group of girls her own age. I think that she found living at home too restrictive and stifling. She transferred to San Diego State and graduated with a degree in accounting. I was so happy when Helene graduated from college—this was a real milestone in our family. I wish that someone from the Wiener family could have seen her graduate.

The last formal education that I had was in Krotoszyn. I never resumed my studies, and the only classes that I took after the war were to learn English and civics in order to pass the citizenship test. I have what you might call "street smarts." Helene really fulfilled a dream that someone in our family might get a college degree. I was so proud of her. When she was growing up, I remember that the extent of our conversations were, "How are your grades?" I did not know anything about education, but I was proud when Helene got good grades. She used to say, "Thank you, Daddy," but she knew that I really did not understand all the courses that she was taking to get her degree. I was happy to give her whatever encouragement and praise she needed.

Helene can do whatever she sets her mind to. For a while she worked for Coldwell Banker and then she worked with me leasing property. When she was 28 years old she met her husband, Jonathan Shapiro, who is a good-natured person, a real mensch. He was in the produce business and when National Lumber went out of business, he took over the space and today manages the swap meet in Fontana. Recently, Helene opened a

Curves franchise, and it is one of the most successful stores in this national fitness chain. Helene and Jon have two children. Shane, who is 13, and just had a wonderful bar mitzvah. I was very proud of him; in his speech he talked about the significance of the Holocaust. His sister, Sydney is 10; she is a very beautiful and charming young girl.

I love all my grandchildren, but I have become more selfish with my time since Renée passed away. It may be my age, but when they say, "Grandpa, let's go to dinner," I am more than happy to be with them. Sydney looks like my sister, Malka; and Shane looks just like his father, Jon. They are both lovable children and I get a lot of pleasure from being with them. We play cards, go shopping, and they used to go swimming at our house in Beverly Hills at 809 North Alta Drive.

When Renée was alive, she devoted her life to our grandchildren. Countless times she used to say to me. "David, you stay home. I'm going to see the children." She had infinite patience with them no matter what they did. On rare occasions she did lose her temper. I remember that Sydney once used crayons on a newly-installed carpet in our house. Renée was very upset and it was the first and only time that I heard her yell at Sydney. I asked Sydney, "Hold it. Do you know what you just did?" She looked at me and said, "Grandpa, I am only four years old; I don't know everything." Renée started to laugh. She was always understanding and compassionate with the grandchildren. They became her whole life.

I call my son, Michael, my Kaddishel. (In Yiddish, this means the son who prays for the soul of his departed father—he repeats the Kaddish, the traditional Jewish prayer for the dead.) When Michael was born, it was a new world. The Wiener name would continue in spite of what Hitler tried to do. Michael went to Yavneh, a Jewish orthodox school on Beverly Boulevard from the time he was five until he was 13 years old. I remember one day Michael forgot to wear his prayer shawl and the rabbi wanted to kick him out of school. Michael called me and told me what the rabbi had threatened to do to him.

I went to the school and confronted the Rabbi. "Rabbi, I am a survivor. I came from a very orthodox home in Lodz. After all that happened to me during the Holocaust and all that I lost, I really don't believe in God. I did not send my son to this school to believe in God—that is his choice. What I want for him is that he understands the Jewish culture and where he came from." The rabbi understood what I meant, and that was the last I heard of any threats against Michael.

When Michael was 12, he spent the summer working for me at Western Fabric. Luis, Victor, and Juan taught him how to drive a forklift which was a big thrill for him, because he did not even have his driver's license. I made sure that the boys watched out for Michael. In later years, Michael has become a big help to me in business, as an advisor, and then as the chief operating officer of our real estate development company.

In 1976, when the family moved to a three-bedroom house on Alta Drive north of Sunset Boulevard, we enrolled the children in the Beverly Hills public schools which were excellent. Michael transferred from Yavneh to the Hawthorne Middle School, and Helene went to Beverly Hills High School. While the children were at school, Renée worked in our garden planting flowers. I really had no interest—I am not a nature boy—but it was something that Renée loved to do. She also devoted a lot of time to Hadassah and on her own supported many different charities. I was unaware of how many organizations she had helped until people came up to me at her memorial service to tell me of her generosity.

Renée and I used to take the family to a resort near Palm Springs when the children were teenagers. The resort was like a dude ranch with horses, a campfire and lots of sports. For breakfast, the ranch served ham and eggs and I ate it in front of the children. Michael said, "Daddy, didn't your father teach you not to eat ham?" At that moment, I felt like I could drop dead on the floor. I said to Michael. "You are right. Why don't we go for a walk after breakfast." I told him some facts about the war. Eating kosher was not an option. You just grabbed anything that you could to survive.

"But if it makes you happy, I will not eat bacon or ham anymore." We shook hands. Michael bought me a trophy inscribed with the words, "My father is the greatest." When Michael went off to college, he started to eat ham but I had made a commitment to him and to this day I will not eat bacon or ham.

Michael was a good student. He graduated summa cum laude and then went on to the University of Oregon to study architecture. He became a real nature boy while he was living in Eugene. He left Oregon to be in San Diego with Helene. He went to a Catholic private school there, University of San Diego. One day, I got a call from Helene, who was sharing an apartment with Michael and a group of other students. "Dad, the landlord wants to kick us out of the apartment." I went down to San Diego and bought them a condominium, and they had a ball together. After finishing school, Michael enrolled in law school at Loyola University. He decided to visit Israel between his first and second year there.

Renée and I started receiving telephone calls from Michael, "Mom and Dad, I am in love." He had met his future wife, Michele Brendel, whose family was originally from Belgium, and by an amazing coincidence, Renée knew her family before the war. Michele was serving in the Israeli army. She and Michael were married in Belgium in a civil ceremony and then had a Jewish wedding in Tel Aviv.

It was during the days that the family spent in Tel Aviv for my son's wedding, that I had an amazing reunion (as has happened to me so many times while visiting Israel). I hailed a taxi outside our hotel and asked the driver, "Where is a good place for falafel?" The driver asked me where I came from, and then inquired, "What were you doing during the war and what is your name?

"My name is Dufce Wiener" and then I told him that I had been imprisoned in Deblin and later Auschwitz. He insisted that "Dufce" was dead. He stopped the taxi and turned around to look at me. "Dufce?"

"Ya, ya."

"It's me! Moshe Salzman!" I could not believe what I was hearing. He was the very same Moshe Salzman who was suspected of stealing the gun that I took from the Gestapo. Later I asked him, "Do you remember the beating you and I took from the Gestapo."

"Yes, I remember that. I still have scars on my back." "Moshe, I was the one who took the gun."

We laughed. He raised a glass of wine and said, "Dufce, we are in Israel. We are alive. Thank God for that. L'Chaim."

Moshe invited Renée and me to his house, and we met his wife and other survivors of Deblin who were still his friends. I listened to them telling stories about me. In the camp, they were all convinced that "Dufce toit" (David is dead) after I escaped with Granek. From the ashes of those horrific events, came great happiness—Moshe and his wife helped us bring together survivors from Deblin to come to the wedding.

The newlyweds came back to the United States so that Michael could finish law school. He then became an associate at a prestigious law firm, Manatt, Phelps and Phillips. His wife, Michele, worked at Bullock's Department Store and took English classes. Michael and Michele have two children: my granddaughter Melanie is 15; she is very conservative, lovable, well behaved, and very serious about her studies. She received her bat mitzvah. In looks, she resembles Michele's family, and like her mother, she is a beautiful, young lady. My 11-year old grandson, Mathieu is handsome and very sure of himself. He is dedicated to sports, especially tennis. He has many of the Wiener family characteristics, including being a big teaser.

In 2001, when I was 75 years old, I decided that it was time to take the entire family to Poland. I thought that it was important for my children and grandchildren to see the remnants of the camps for themselves, to know what had happened to me during the Holocaust, and to visit the places where I had lived with my family before the war. I wanted them to know more about the Wiener family history.

In Warsaw, I showed my children and grandchildren every street where I lived in the ghetto and described to them the terrible sight of bodies covered in brown paper lying in the streets. From there we traveled to my hometown of Lodz. I pointed out where my family's apartment had been and where the synagogue had stood. Everything was gone. Not one brick was left of the beautiful sanctuary where Moshe Chaim prayed each and every day of his life. Seeing that empty place brought back memories of my mother crying in the synagogue in the upper balcony. I remember asking my brother Yosel why my mother used to cry. "She is asking for forgiveness for her children's sins."

"For what?"

He would tell me, "She prays to God that if one of her children is ill, God will not punish her child. He should punish her for whatever she might have done to bring this upon her child." My mother used to say, "My poor child is innocent. Punish me." My mother would take the bread out of her own mouth to feed any of her children. I told my family these stories so that they would know who Hannah Wiener was—an angel.

I rented a mini-bus with a chauffeur and an interpreter to take us around Lodz to visit the places where some of my brothers had lived. At Ul Dzielna 21, my brother Szyje had a little tailor shop where he made beautiful clothes for wealthy ladies. Sometimes I would help him iron the clothes and he would pay me a few cents. We found his house and there was a swastika on the door in the hallway of the building. It did not really surprise me that there was still so much anti-Semitism in Poland even when there are but a handful of Jews living there today. We drove through the district of Kilensko, where my brother Yitzchak, who was an accountant, had an office and apartment where he lived with his wife.

Then we went to the Jewish cemetery in Lodz where my father is buried. I had been there two years earlier. At that time, I tried to get a minyan to stand with me at his grave to say Kaddish, but I could not find ten Jewish men in the entire city.

When we reached my father's grave, I told Renée and the children that I needed to be alone. I thought about the last time that I saw my father alive—how he could not say goodbye to me on the day that I escaped from the Lodz ghetto. I think that he was heart-broken, but he knew that he was not going to leave his home, his wife, his daughter, or his youngest son, Mendel. That decision certainly sealed their fate.

Finally, I spoke to my father standing over his grave. I told him, "Moshe Chaim, you have a grandson, Michael, who is named after you, and a granddaughter, Helene, who is named after Mother, and you have four wonderful great grandchildren. They are all the new branches of our family." Sometime later, I ordered a plaque for my father's grave which was added to the original Hebrew inscription and made sure that his gravesite is properly maintained. I visit the cemetery as often as I can.

The plaque reads:

In Loving Memory
Of Beloved Parents
Father, Moshe Chaim
Mother, Chana Sura
Their Children, Wiener Family Members
Szyje and his wife,
Malka and her husband, Rachmil Schwartzberg
Yitzchak and his wife
Yosel, Yidel, Welfrel and Mendel
Who were murdered by the German Nazis during the
Second World War, 1941-1944.

This plaque was placed here by their only surviving son,
David Wiener, and his wife, children and grandchildren of the U.S.A.

I never found out where my mother is buried, although I wrote many letters to Jewish organizations that tried to help survivors find members of their family.

From Lodz we traveled to Krotoszyn where I lived with my oldest brother, Jacob, and his wife, Irene at Ul Krotka 2. I remembered the little garden that I took care of, and my beautiful Aunt Irene who treated me as if I were her own son. Two families were living in what used to be our house. The synagogue where her father served as the cantor had disappeared.

I stopped a man on the street and asked if he knew where the Marshal Josef Pilsudski School is. "What does it look like?" I told him that it was made of red brick. He took us there, but the building was locked. I found a caretaker and he let us in. Nothing had changed since 1939. The principal's office was just where it had been. I recalled standing in front of the class as the teacher warned the students that one day I would cheat them; the heavy-set principal hitting me on the hands for getting into a fight with the Christian boys who had attacked me for being Jewish; sitting in the front row of the classroom; and singing in the boys' choir. I relived the moment when my teacher told me to donate my bicycle to the Polish army and handed me a piece of yellow paper so that I could redeem it after the war. I told my grandchildren all these stories.

In Deblin, I wanted to find the Gestapo bunker where I worked outside the ghetto. I knew it was on the main street but I did not know the exact location. I saw an old man about my age wearing worn-out slippers walking haltingly. I asked him, "Do you know where the Gestapo headquarters were on this street?"

He answered "Ya, ya," and then he pointed to the exact spot where I had built the bunker to protect the Gestapo from air attacks by the Russians. I had been put in charge of the cement mixer, and the head of the Gestapo, Knaphaider, used to watch me. He eventually saved my life for no other reason than that I was a hard worker. When the selection was made to send Jews to the concentration camp, Knaphaider pulled me out of the line that was destined for Treblinka and assigned me to the workers' line. I wanted to show this place to my family and tell them how I survived but sometimes I don't even believe that these things actually happened to me.

We also went to Auschwitz. The hands of the clock in my mind turned back to 1944. Walking through the darkened Block 11, Block 8, Block 5, and Block 4—all the sections of the camp where I was imprisoned—I felt numb, cold, without feeling. Standing in the barracks next to the barbed wire, I remembered the blackened corpses, my fellow inmates starving for a piece of bread, a cup of watery soup—anything to fill our swollen bellies. For a while, I was not aware of my family around me. I was just alone with my memories. The world did not exist for me. Then my grandson, Shane, ran up to me. He grabbed my legs from behind. "Grandpa, I feel your pain." With that gesture and compassionate comment, he brought me back to the present. I turned around and asked my daughter, "Helene, did you say anything to Shane?" She said no. I looked at my family, all standing there beside me, and thought, "Thank God, we live in America and I have a family again."

The whole trip through Poland took seven days. I can still remember every street, the number of every apartment where my brothers lived as if it were yesterday. Even in the best of times, I was a tenant in Poland; it was never really a home. We, as Jews, were never accepted there and after the war had ended, the Poles did what they could to annihilate the few Jews who came back to find any family members who had survived the war.

Even after this trip I am not really sure that my children and grandchildren can truly understand what happened during the Holocaust. If you have not been through the same thing, it is hard to imagine what it was really like. That is one of the reasons that survivors get together. We share a common history. We really have no tears left—just pain, and we understand each other's pain. To this day, I can see someone walking down the street and I can tell if he is a survivor. There is something in his face, something different, something that has marked him.

chapter thirteen

DON'T FORGET TO
LOOK AT THE MOON

Renée and I celebrated our 50th wedding anniversary by renewing our wedding vows in October 2001. It was my idea to throw a lavish party at the Four Seasons Hotel in Beverly Hills for our family and over 300 guests. Renée wore a beautiful white dress, and I had on a tuxedo. It was not easy convincing Renée do to this because she never liked to show off, but I thought that it was a fitting celebration of our marriage and our happiness together, after the early years of struggle and heartache. Rabbi Leopold Schneer, who had presided over Helene and Michael's weddings, performed the ceremony. He was a friend of Renée's during her school days in Belgium. It was so wonderful to be surrounded by family and friends and to feel loved and respected.

After the ceremony, we took Helene and Michael, their spouses, and our grandchildren on a trip to Acapulco, Mexico to celebrate. I gave Renée a birthday card which I still have. I wrote, "I love you, Renée. Please, let me die before you." I could not imagine life without her. And then on January 3, 2002, shortly after her 75th birthday on December 25th, and right after returning from our family trip, Renée died under tragic circumstances. The whole world changed for me. I lost my wife, my best friend, my confidante, my true partner in life.

I really could not take care of myself. I felt like I was a "walking dead person." I moved in with Helene, Jonathan, and their children. I lived with them for six months. My granddaughter, Sydney, who was just six years old at the time, gave up her room so that I had a place to stay. She showed great understanding, way beyond her years. She used to comb my hair and wash my face. After the sudden loss of my wife, I think I was in a state of shock and depression. I felt totally empty and kept on thinking, "Why me? Why me? God, what do you want from me? I have already paid my dues."

Staying with Helene and Jon really saved my life. The whole family comforted me. The children showed me how much they loved me. Before I moved out, Sydney and Shane said, "Grandpa, please stay with us. Don't leave. We love you."

I told them, "No. It is time for me to be on my own."

They argued with me and Sydney said, "Grandpa, I don't mind giving up my room for you."

I went to a bereavement group at UCLA a few times, but I really did not have the patience for it. Then my son, Michael, convinced me to see a psychiatrist. She was a very nice lady. I saw her three or four times. At our last session together, she said, "David, sit down. Let me talk to you. You are a very intelligent person. You don't really need me. You have two choices. You can sit in a chair, eat, and die. Or you are going to live."

I stood up from the chair, "Thank you very much, Doctor. I want to live." Even after that session, sometimes I did things that showed that I still did not completely accept Renée's death. I would go out for dinner with another couple and make a reservation for four, instead of three, or I would drive to our house in Beverly Hills, and have to be reminded that I no longer lived there.

For the first year after Renée died, I lit a candle every night in her honor, and I did not go out with another woman. But life has to go on. After a year, I agreed to meet some ladies, but nobody came into my heart. At first, I would invite a lady out for dinner, but I was advised not to do this. One of the support organizations that helped me said, "Just invite someone to breakfast, or coffee, or lunch. Make it quick. Then if you like the person, you can invite her to dinner on the next date." One lady I met tried to impress me with her wealth. She was a beautiful girl, but her money meant nothing to me and I was really disenchanted with her.

Then a friend of mine said, "I have a nice lady for you. Her name is Lila Gilbert. Here is her telephone number. Give her a call." I tried to get in touch with Lila three or four times, leaving messages that were never returned. I thought to myself, "Forget about it." And then she called me. I was getting pretty savvy about this dating business. I said, "You must be very busy. Why don't we just meet for breakfast? We have nothing to lose. If we don't like each other, it's just 'goodbye Charlie.'"

When Lila walked into Jerry's Deli, I felt a connection right away. We had a lot in common. She was from Latvia and her husband had recently died. She brought some photographs with her of people that we knew in common. I felt very comfortable with her. We started going out together. At the time, I was living by myself in a condominium on Maple Drive in Beverly Hills not far from my office. I cannot deny that I felt very lonely and Lila is very good company.

At first, my daughter, Helene had a hard time accepting Lila. When she heard that we were going to Palm Springs together, she was very angry with me. Sometime later, she apologized to me. I told her, "Helene, you have become a very mature woman." Both Helene and Michael approve of Lila which is important to me.

Shortly after Lila and I met, I had plans to go on a cruise over New Year's with a group of friends that did not include Lila. She wanted to say goodbye to me. We met at Factor's Deli. She handed me a little package with toothpaste and other items that I might need for the trip, and then she said, "David, don't forget to look at the moon." Lila really understood me and she helped to fill the empty place in my heart. It is very tough to be by yourself in this life.

My children, Helene and Michael, gave me an 80th birthday party at the Peninsula Hotel in Beverly Hills. The room was filled with survivor friends, business associates, and my loyal staff at DW Development. The Skye Michaels orchestra played wonderful dance music, and at my request some old Yiddish songs. As the evening wore on, I got up the nerve to sing and my grandson, Shane, joined me. He is a real ham and loves to perform.

I work hard to push away the bad thoughts that still interrupt my sleep, and stay awake for the good dreams that fill my life.

On November 30, 2006, Lila and I were married at City Hall in Beverly Hills. Michael, Helene, and their spouses witnessed the ceremony and gave their approval of our marriage. If the marriage does not work out I can blame them. Lila and I honeymooned in Hawaii and then we took the whole family for a New Year's trip to Mexico.

As in any new marriage, we are learning to accommodate one another. Lila is doing a much better job than I am, and I am thankful to her for recognizing my mishigas and idiosyncrasies. At 80 years old, I am in a new marriage, and thinking about new business ventures. I have a lot left that I want to accomplish, and I hope that my beloved parents, Moshe and Hannah are proud of their son, David, and that my children and grandchildren know how much I love them. It is a word that is much easier for me to say these days.

epilogue

A JOKE TO HIDE THE TEARS

I am not a psychologist or a philosopher. I cannot explain the propensity of the Jewish people to write good comedy, to be great standup comedians and to appreciate a good joke—most of us do. I cannot resist repeating a joke that recently came across the Internet. It embodies much of what I believe and I share it with you.

Bill Gates decides to organize an enormous session to recruit a chairman of Microsoft Europe. The 5,000 candidates are all assembled in a large room. One of the candidates is Maurice Cohen, a Parisian Jew, whose family came from Tunisia.

Bill Gates thanks all the candidates for coming and asks that all those who do not know JAVA program language to rise and leave. 2,000 people rise and leave the room.

Maurice Cohen says to himself, "I do not know this language but what have I got to lose if I stay? I'll give it a try."

Bill Gates asks all the candidates that those who have never had the experience of team management of more than 100 people to rise and leave.

2,000 people rise and leave the room.

Maurice Cohen says to himself, "I have never managed anybody but myself but what have I got to lose if I stay? What can happen to me?" So he stays.

Then Bill Gates asks all the candidates who do not have business management diplomas to rise and leave. 500 people rise and leave the room.

Maurice Cohen says to himself, "I left school at the age of 15 but what have I got to lose if I stay?" So he stays in the room.

Lastly, Bill Gates asks all of the candidates who do not speak the Serbo-Croat language to rise and leave. 498 people rise and leave the room.

Maurice Cohen says to himself, "I do not speak Serbo-Croat but what the hell! What have I got to lose?" So he stays in the room. He finds himself alone with one other candidate. Everyone else has gone.

Bill Gates joins them and says, "Apparently, you are the only two candidates who speak Serb-Croatian, so I'd now like to hear you both have a little conversation in that language!"

Calmly, Maurice turns to the other candidate and says to him, "Baruch ata Adonai." The other candidate answers, "Eloheinu melech haolam."

My wife to be, Renée Freilich, and me, two weeks before
our wedding on October 20, 1951.

My certificate of naturalization, November 6, 1952.

Renée's certificate of naturalization, July 6, 1956.

Renée and our children, Helene and Michael, on their way to synagogue.

My brother, Jacob, preparing to sing with the cantor during Yom Kippur services at a synagogue in the San Fernando Valley shortly before he died (1970).

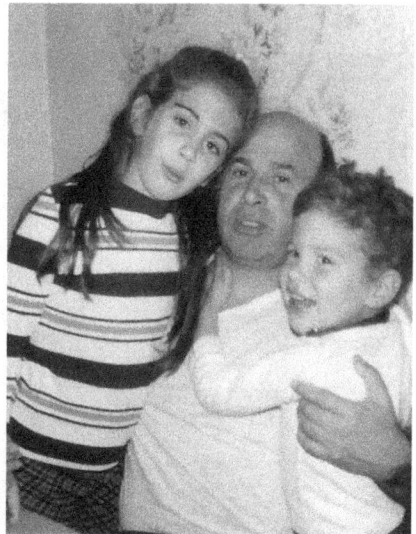

Helene, age 8, and Michael, age 5 with their proud Papa.

Renée and I are in Israel, 1977, shortly after the Yom Kippur War.

Grandma and Grandpa Wiener with our daughter, Helene,
and grandchildren, Shane and Sydney.

On a busy street in Lodz, Poland. I am there with Renée, my children, their spouses, and Shane and Sydney (1998).

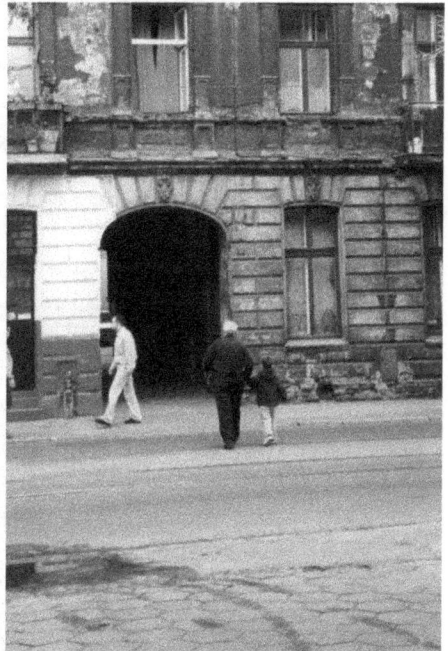

Shane and I are walking toward the building at UI Dzielna 21 where my brother, Szyje, had a tailor shop.

I found the remains of the Gestapo bunker which I built during the war outside the wall of the Deblin ghetto.

The classroom in the Joseph Pilsudki School where my teacher warned my classmates about me because I was a "clever Jew."

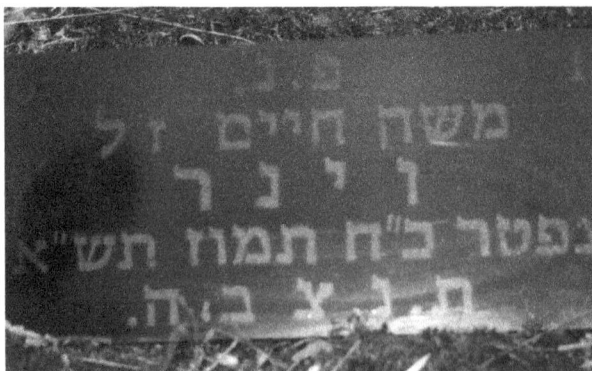

My father's grave in the Lodz cemetery. The original inscription is in ancient Hebrew and reads: "Moshe Chaim Wiener passed away on the 28th of the month of Tammuz, 5701. May his righteous soul be bound in eternal life."

Renée and I meeting Colonel Ilan Ramon, Israel's first astronaut, who perished in the Space Shuttle Columbia Disaster a few years later. We were in Los Angeles at a meeting of the 1939 Club, Survivors of the Holocaust.

Renée and I have a second wedding ceremony on our 50th wedding anniversary at the Four Seasons in Beverly Hills. To our left are my daughter, Helene, and her husband, Jonathan Shapiro and to our right are my son, Michael, and his wife, Michele. In front of us are (left to right) grandchildren Shane and Sydney Shapiro, Melanie and Mathieu Wiener (October 2001).

Shane at his bar mitzvah
holding the Torah with a special
Auschwitz remembrance cover
(April 2006).

Lila Gilbert and me with other
supporters of the Young Artists
International in Israel (2006).

Surrounded by soldiers, the backbone of Israel (2006).

Lila, my future wife, and me at my 80th birthday party.

Looking forward to the future.

www.ingramcontent.com/pod-product-compliance
Lightning Source LLC
LaVergne TN
LVHW041226080426
835508LV00011B/1095